JOHNS HOPKINS
MEDICINE

Prostate Disorders

Your personal guide to prevention, diagnosis and treatment

H. Ballentine Carter, M.D.

2012

The Johns Hopkins White Papers are a series of disease-specific publications designed for health care consumers with chronic conditions who desire accurate, comprehensive and easy-to-understand information to enable them to better manage their disorder. Each White Paper is prepared in consultation with one or more specialists from Johns Hopkins Medicine. A new, updated edition of each White Paper is released each January and sold throughout the year.

The White Papers are produced in partnership with Remedy Health Media, LLC. For information on our complete line of Johns Hopkins health publications—our White Papers and Digital Special Reports, our Prostate and Memory Bulletins, and our monthly Health After 50 newsletter—please visit our website: **www.JohnsHopkinsHealthAlerts.com.**

Basic price: $39.95

ISBN 978-1-935584-59-9

Printed in the United States of America

The information contained in this White Paper is not intended as a substitute for the advice of a physician. Readers who suspect they may have specific medical problems should consult a physician about any suggestions made.

The Johns Hopkins White Papers

Esther Benenson
Editor in Chief, Digital & Print
Johns Hopkins Publications

Beverly Lucas
Executive Editor

Gerald Secor Couzens
Staff Writer

Tim Gower
Editorial Research

Tim Jeffs
Creative Director

Dragonfly Media Group
Medical Illustrations

Joyce Ippolito
Michael Kaufman
Copy Editors

Remedy Health Media, LLC

Traver Hutchins
Chairman

Michael Cunnion
Chief Executive Officer

David Lee
Executive Vice President, Publishing

Patrick Aysseh
Executive Vice President, Digital

Lisa Cohen
Chief Financial Officer

Table of Contents

Introducing Your
Prostate Disorders Expert

The Johns Hopkins Hospital is No. 1 in the United States for urology, according to *U.S. News & World Report's* Best Hospitals rankings for 2011-12. Your Johns Hopkins expert for the Prostate Disorders White Paper is Dr. H. Ballentine Carter.

H. Ballentine Carter, M.D., is Professor of Urology and Oncology and the Director of Adult Urology at the Johns Hopkins University School of Medicine. He has written extensively on the diagnosis and staging of prostate cancer. In particular, he has researched prostate-specific antigen (PSA) levels: how they change as men age; their variability in men with prostate cancer; and their use in staging, predicting and managing prostate cancer. Currently, he is working closely with the Baltimore Longitudinal Study of Aging to evaluate the development of prostate disease with age. In addition, he began what is now the largest active surveillance program for prostate cancer in the United States to monitor men with prostate cancer who do not need immediate treatment. Dr. Carter has had research articles published in *The Journal of Urology, Urology, Cancer Research,* the *Journal of the American Medical Association* and the *Journal of the National Cancer Institute.*

Prostate Disorders

The prostate is a gland located at the base of a man's bladder, behind the pubic bone and in front of the rectum. This gland, roughly the size and shape of a small crab apple, weighs only about an ounce in young men. It surrounds the urethra, the tube that carries urine away from the bladder and transports semen during ejaculation (see "The Anatomy of the Prostate" on page 3). A good way to envision the prostate is as an apple with the core removed, with the urethra passing through the middle.

The prostate's primary function is to produce prostatic fluid, a component of semen. Also, during ejaculation, smooth muscles in the prostate contract to help propel semen through the urethra.

Technically the prostate is not part of the urinary system. But because of its location and relationship to the urethra, the prostate can (and often does) affect urinary function.

Benign prostatic enlargement

When a man reaches his mid-40s, the area of the prostate that encircles the urethra begins to grow. This overgrowth of prostate tissue is called benign prostatic enlargement (BPE), also known as benign prostatic hyperplasia (BPH). With continued growth, the expanding prostate may constrict the urethra, causing symptoms such as difficulty starting urination or a weak urine stream.

BPE occurs in approximately 31 percent of men between the ages of 50 and 59, 36 percent of men age 60 to 69, and 44 percent of those who are age 70 and older. Not all of these men experience urinary tract problems related to BPE but many do. Although BPE can cause a number of bothersome symptoms, it is not life threatening.

Prostate cancer

Cancer of the prostate is a much more serious health problem than BPE. After skin cancer, it is the second most common cancer in American men and is second only to lung cancer as a cause of cancer deaths. In 2010, an estimated 218,000 men were diagnosed with prostate cancer, and about 33,000 died of the disease, according to the American Cancer Society.

The good news is that today, reliable diagnostic tests and numerous treatment options are available, and death rates from prostate cancer are now on the decline. Nearly 100 percent of men are still alive five years after a prostate cancer diagnosis, more than 93 percent are alive 10 years after diagnosis, and approximately 79 percent are alive 15 years after diagnosis.

Prostate cancer rarely causes symptoms until far advanced. By contrast, BPE commonly causes urinary symptoms. Having BPE neither increases nor decreases a man's risk of prostate cancer. However, it is possible for a man to have both conditions at the same time.

Prostatitis

Also known as inflammation of the prostate, prostatitis is a common and often frustrating problem, particularly when the cause is not obvious. It can cause pain in the lower back and in the area between the scrotum and rectum (the perineum) and may be accompanied by chills, fever and a general feeling of malaise when caused by bacteria. The most common type—nonbacterial prostatitis—can cause chronic symptoms including perineal discomfort, postejaculatory pain and urination symptoms—characterized by periods of improvement and worsening.

Structure of the Prostate

The prostate is made up of three kinds of cells: glandular (epithelial) cells, smooth muscle cells and stromal cells. The glandular cells produce part of the prostatic fluid. The smooth muscles contract to push prostatic fluid into the urethra during ejaculation. Smooth muscles are involuntary, which means they are not under the conscious control of the individual. Stromal cells make up the support structure of the prostate.

The prostate can be divided into three main regions or zones. Immediately surrounding the urethra is the transition zone. In this zone is the tissue that begins to grow in BPE. Next is the central zone, which contains a portion of the prostate's glandular tissue. The largest and outermost region is the peripheral zone, the area containing the largest proportion of glandular tissue and the site where most prostate cancers develop (see "The Anatomy of the Prostate" on page 3).

The Anatomy of the Prostate

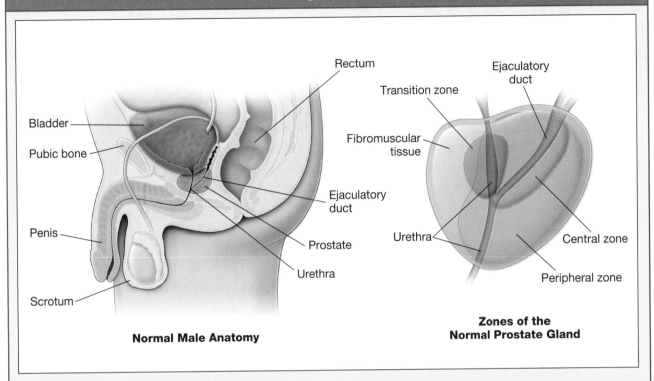

Normal Male Anatomy

Zones of the
Normal Prostate Gland

Many men are not aware of the location and function of their prostate gland until it begins to cause health problems. The gland is chestnut shaped and sits at the base of the bladder, in front of the rectum and behind the base of the penis. It produces prostatic fluid (a component of semen), functions as a valve to keep urine and sperm flowing in the proper direction, and pumps semen into the urethra during orgasm. The gland is about the size of a pea at birth and grows until it reaches its normal adult size (roughly 1.5 inches in diameter) in a man's early 20s. When a man reaches his mid-40s or later, the inner portion of the prostate tends to enlarge, a condition called benign prostatic enlargement, or BPE (also referred to as benign prostatic hyperplasia, or BPH).

Physicians usually divide the prostate into three main zones (see illustration on right). The peripheral zone comprises the outermost portion of the prostate gland and accounts for about 70 percent of its volume. Because prostate cancer is most likely to develop in this area, doctors usually sample tissue from this section during a biopsy. Since much of the peripheral zone sits adjacent to the rectum, doctors can often detect prostate cancer with a digital rectal exam.

The transition zone is the innermost section of the prostate gland and accounts for roughly 5 percent of its volume in a healthy man. This zone surrounds the urethra, which passes from the bladder to the penis through the prostate. BPE begins in the tissues of the transition zone. Enlargement of this zone constricts the urethra and leads to the urination problems that are common in men with BPE.

The central zone, which sits between the peripheral and transition zones, makes up about 25 percent of the gland's volume. The ejaculatory ducts, through which semen enters the urethra, pass through this zone. Prostate cancer and BPE are unlikely to develop in the central zone. ■

BENIGN PROSTATIC ENLARGEMENT

Benign prostatic enlargement (BPE)—also known as benign prostatic hyperplasia (BPH)—is the most common benign (noncancerous) growth process in men. As is true for prostate cancer, BPE occurs more often in Western industrialized countries (the United States, the United Kingdom and Canada, for example) than in Eastern countries (such as Japan and China). BPE appears to be more common among black men than among white men, and some evidence suggests that a family history of BPE may increase the risk. Being overweight, especially with extra fat concentrated around the abdomen, increases the risk of developing BPE.

More than 50 percent of men over age 50 and 80 percent of those over 80 experience some BPE-related symptoms. Treatment for the condition is necessary only if symptoms begin to interfere with a man's quality of life. The main treatment options for BPE include medications that either shrink the prostate or relax the muscle tissue that constricts the urethra; surgery to remove, ablate or vaporize excess prostate tissue; and heat therapy called thermotherapy.

Causes of BPE

In BPE, prostate cells accumulate and the organ tissue becomes overgrown, or enlarged. Tissue overgrowth produces nodules in the transition zone of the prostate. The increase in prostate cells is due to a slowing of apoptosis (normal programmed cell death), not because of an increase in cell production.

What triggers BPE is not well understood, but aging and testosterone (the predominant male sex hormone) are believed to be the primary influences on its development. Animal studies suggest that the female sex hormone estrogen (produced in small amounts in men) also may play a role, perhaps when a man's testosterone production declines and the balance of the two hormones is altered.

Symptoms of BPE

BPE symptoms arise only when the expanding nodules of prostate tissue (and the tightening of smooth muscle) place enough pressure on the urethra to interfere with urine flow. But some men whose prostate is very enlarged may not have urethral obstruction;

What's Your Prostate Symptom Score?

Calculating whether you need treatment for BPE

The questionnaire used for the International Prostate Symptom Score (see below) was developed to help men evaluate the severity of their symptoms from benign prostatic enlargement (BPE). This self-administered test can help you determine which type of treatment is needed, if any. Use your total score to assess BPE severity: mild (1 to 7), moderate (8 to 19), or severe (20 to 35).

Generally, no treatment is needed if symptoms are mild; moderate symptoms usually call for some form of treatment; and severe symptoms indicate that surgery is most likely to be effective. ■

Circle one number on each line and tabulate your total score.

	Not at all	Less than 1 time in 5	Less than half the time	About half the time	More than half the time	Almost always
1. Over the past month, how often have you had the sensation of not emptying your bladder completely after you finished urinating?	0	1	2	3	4	5
2. Over the past month, how often have you had to urinate again less than two hours after you finished urinating?	0	1	2	3	4	5
3. Over the past month, how often have you found you stopped and started again several times when you urinated?	0	1	2	3	4	5
4. Over the past month, how often have you found it difficult to postpone urination?	0	1	2	3	4	5
5. Over the past month, how often have you had a weak urinary stream?	0	1	2	3	4	5
6. Over the past month, how often have you had to push or strain to begin urination?	0	1	2	3	4	5

	None	1 time	2 times	3 times	4 times	5x or more
7. Over the past month, how many times did you most typically get up to urinate from the time you went to bed at night until the time you got up in the morning?	0	1	2	3	4	5

Total Score: _____

Source: American Urological Association.

abdomen is checked for the presence of a mass, which could indicate an enlarged bladder due to retained urine. A digital rectal exam (DRE) is performed to assess the size, shape and consistency of the prostate. This examination, which involves the insertion of a gloved, lubricated finger into the rectum, is mildly uncomfortable but extremely important. Detection of hard or firm areas in the prostate raises the suspicion of prostate cancer.

If an individual's medical history suggests neurological disease, the physician may look for abnormalities such as a loss of sensation or weakness in the lower body, which may indicate that the urinary symptoms are due to a neurogenic bladder.

Frequency/Volume Chart

A frequency/volume chart may provide the doctor with important information about your condition, especially if nocturia (frequent night-time urination) is the main symptom. To use a frequency/ volume chart, a man needs to record the time and amount of urine he passes each time he urinates over the course of several days. The doctor will provide instructions regarding how to collect and measure the urine.

Laboratory Tests

Urinalysis—examination of a urine sample under a microscope—is performed in all patients who have lower urinary tract symptoms. Urinalysis is often the only laboratory test needed when symptoms are mild (International Prostate Symptom Score of 1 to 7) and the medical history and physical examination suggest no other abnormalities.

A urine culture (an attempt to grow and identify bacteria in a laboratory dish) is performed when a urinary tract infection is suspected. In the presence of severe or chronic symptoms of BPE, blood tests to detect abnormalities in creatinine, blood urea nitrogen and hemoglobin are used to rule out the presence of kidney damage or anemia.

A prostate-specific antigen (PSA) test is generally recommended (see discussion on pages 31-36). PSA values alone are not helpful in determining whether symptoms are due to BPE or prostate cancer because both conditions can cause elevated levels. However, knowing a man's PSA level may help predict how rapidly his prostate will increase in size over time and whether problems such as urinary retention are likely to occur.

Special Diagnostic Tests

Men who experience moderate to severe symptoms (International Prostate Symptom Score of 8 or higher) may benefit from one or more of the following tests: uroflowmetry, pressure-flow urodynamic studies, imaging studies or cystoscopy.

Uroflowmetry

In this noninvasive test, a man urinates into an electronic device that measures the speed of his urine flow. A slow flow rate suggests an obstruction of the urethra. If the flow rate is high, urethral obstruction is unlikely and therapy for BPE will not be effective in most instances. The average urine flow rate for a man over age 45 is 12 mL per second.

Pressure-flow urodynamic studies

These studies measure bladder pressure during urination by placing a recording device into the bladder and often into the rectum. The difference in pressure between the bladder and the rectum indicates the pressure generated when the bladder muscle contracts. A high pressure accompanied by a low urine flow rate indicates urethral obstruction. A low pressure with a low urine flow rate signals an abnormality in the bladder itself, such as one related to a neurological disorder.

Imaging studies

In general, imaging studies are done only in patients who have blood in their urine, a urinary tract infection, abnormal kidney function, previous urinary tract surgery or a history of urinary tract stones.

Ultrasonography is the imaging study used most often in men with lower urinary tract symptoms. The test involves pressing a microphone-sized device (transducer) onto the skin of the lower abdomen. As the device is passed over the area, it emits sound waves that reflect off the internal organs. The pattern of the reflected sound waves is used to create an image of each organ. Ultrasonography can be used to detect structural abnormalities in the kidneys or bladder, determine the amount of residual urine in the bladder, detect the presence of bladder stones and estimate the size of the prostate.

Less frequently, another imaging study, intravenous pyelography, may be performed. This procedure involves injecting a dye into a vein and taking X-rays of the urinary tract. The dye makes urine visible on the X-rays and shows any urinary tract obstructions or stones.

Cystoscopy

In this procedure, a cystoscope (a small lighted viewing device) is passed through the urethra into the bladder to directly view the two structures. Cystoscopy is usually performed just before prostate surgery to guide the surgeon in performing the procedure or to look for abnormalities of the urethra or bladder.

When Is Treatment for BPE Necessary?

Unfortunately, the progression of BPE cannot be predicted with accuracy. Symptoms and objective measurements of urethral obstruction can remain stable for many years and may even improve over time in as many as a third of men. In a large evaluation of BPE treatments, called the Medical Therapy of Prostatic Symptoms (MTOPS) study, only 14 percent of untreated men in the placebo group experienced worsening symptoms during an average follow-up time of 4.5 years.

Men who eventually need treatment for BPE typically experience a progressive decrease in the size and force of their urinary stream or a sensation of incomplete emptying of their bladder. Although frequent nighttime urination is one of the most annoying symptoms of BPE, it does not predict the need for future treatment.

If urethral obstruction worsens and is left untreated, complications can occur. Potential complications include a thickened bladder with a reduced ability to store urine, infected residual urine, bladder stones, and a backup of pressure that damages the kidneys.

Treatment decisions for BPE are based on the severity of symptoms as assessed by the International Prostate Symptom Score questionnaire (see "What's Your Prostate Symptom Score?" on page 7), the extent of urinary tract damage, and the man's age and overall health. In general, no treatment is needed for men who have only a few symptoms and are not bothered by them. Treatment—usually surgery—is required when there is kidney damage due to inadequate bladder emptying; a complete inability to urinate after treatment of acute urinary retention; incontinence due to overfilling or increased bladder sensitivity; bladder stones; infected residual urine; recurrent blood in the urine despite treatment with medication; or symptoms that have not responded to medication and are troublesome enough to diminish quality of life.

Treatment decisions are most difficult for men who have moderate symptoms (International Prostate Symptom Score of 8 to 19). Each of these men must determine whether the symptoms bother him enough or interfere with his life enough to merit treatment.

Treatment Options for BPE

The main treatment options for BPE are watchful waiting (close monitoring but no immediate treatment), plant-based remedies (phytotherapy), medication, surgery and minimally invasive procedures. If medications do not relieve symptoms in a man who is not a candidate for surgery (for example, because he is unable to withstand the rigors of surgery), urethral obstruction and incontinence may be managed with intermittent catheterization or with an indwelling Foley catheter (a catheter with a balloon at its tip that, when inflated, holds the catheter in place in the bladder). The catheter is usually changed monthly.

Watchful Waiting

Because the course of BPE is unpredictable, watchful waiting is the best option for men with minimal symptoms that are not especially bothersome. With this management option, physician visits are needed about once a year to review symptom status, conduct a physical examination and perform a few simple laboratory tests.

During watchful waiting, men should adopt certain lifestyle measures to help relieve symptoms or prevent them from worsening. For example, they should not take over-the-counter antihistamines or decongestants and should avoid delaying urination. They also need to limit the amount of fluid consumed at any one time and not drink anything after 7 P.M.

In addition, they should avoid beverages that contain caffeine, limit alcohol intake, and cut back on spicy or salty foods. Engaging in regular physical activity, doing Kegel exercises (see page 68) and keeping warm also can be helpful. The association between lower urinary tract symptoms and cold weather is probably related to increased sympathetic activity (the sympathetic nervous system is more active in cold weather), which causes increased smooth muscle tone within the prostate. Preventing weight gain (especially around the middle), eating a diet rich in vegetables, and keeping blood sugar under control may help reduce lower urinary tract symptoms.

Phytotherapy

Some people elect to use dietary supplements that contain plant-derived substances or minerals to manage their symptoms. Saw palmetto is the most well-known remedy, but African plum, trinovin, South African star grass, flower pollen extract, soy, stinging nettle, rye pollen, purple cone flower and pumpkin seeds also are used to manage BPE symptoms, as are supplements of the minerals zinc and selenium.

A dietary supplement called beta-sitosterol has shown some benefits in BPE, including improvements in urinary symptoms and urine flow rates. However, well-conducted studies of beta-sitosterol are limited. In contrast, an analysis of 21 well-conducted studies of saw palmetto (including more than 3,000 men with BPE) found that

LATEST RESEARCH

New warning about 5-ARIs

If you use finasteride (Proscar) or dutasteride (Avodart) for benign prostatic enlargement (BPE), you may have noticed a new warning on the accompanying drug information sheet. Both drugs are 5-alpha-reductase inhibitors (ARIs), and the Food and Drug Administration (FDA) is requiring their manufacturers to warn 5-ARI users that the drugs are associated with a small but increased risk of aggressive prostate cancer. The warning also pertains to Propecia, the baldness drug that contains a low dose of finasteride, and the combination BPE drug Jalyn, which contains dutasteride and tamsulosin.

The label change was based on the FDA's review of two large, randomized controlled trials that evaluated the potential of Proscar and Avodart to reduce the risk of prostate cancer. They found that men taking either medication had a lower incidence of lower-risk prostate cancer, but a higher risk for high-grade prostate cancer.

The FDA believes that 5-ARIs are safe and effective for BPE. But, if you're taking one, talk to your doctor about how often you should be screened for prostate cancer. Keep in mind that 5-ARIs decrease serum PSA levels by approximately 50 percent. Therefore, any confirmed increase in PSA—even if the value is within the normal range—calls for careful follow-up by your doctor to rule out the presence of prostate cancer.

FOOD AND DRUG ADMINISTRATION
June 2011

supplement users were 76 percent more likely to have experienced symptom improvement than men taking a placebo. However, a randomized trial published in the *New England Journal of Medicine* found no significant differences in symptoms between men taking saw palmetto and those taking a placebo. The adverse effects related to saw palmetto are usually mild and infrequent. They include headache, dizziness, nausea and mild abdominal pain.

If saw palmetto is going to work, it usually does so within the first month. Therefore, supplements should be stopped if symptoms do not improve after a month of use.

If the supplements relieve your symptoms, you may want to continue taking them, but inform your doctor that you are doing so. The typical dose is 160 mg taken twice a day. Supplements that contain at least 85 percent free fatty acids and at least 0.2 percent sterols are the most likely to be effective.

Medication

The two types of drugs most commonly used to treat BPE are alpha-1-adrenergic blockers (alpha-blockers) and 5-alpha-reductase inhibitors. Research suggests that these drugs improve symptoms in 30 to 60 percent of men. However, it is not possible to predict who will respond to medication or which drug will work best for a particular person.

Alpha-1-adrenergic blockers

Alpha-blockers relax smooth muscle tissue within the prostate by blocking the effect of nerve impulses that signal the muscles to contract. As a result, daily use of an alpha-blocker may increase urinary flow and relieve urinary frequency, urinary urgency and frequent nighttime urination. Currently, several alpha-blockers are used to treat BPE. These include alfuzosin (Uroxatral), doxazosin (Cardura), tamsulosin (Flomax) and terazosin (Hytrin).

One advantage of alpha-blockers over 5-alpha-reductase inhibitors (discussed on page 14) is that they work almost immediately. In addition, they can treat high blood pressure (hypertension) in men with that condition. However, whether alpha-blockers are superior to 5-alpha-reductase inhibitors may depend more on the size of the prostate. In one comparison study, Hytrin appeared to produce greater improvement in BPE symptoms and urinary flow rate than Proscar. But this difference may have been due to the larger number of men with small prostates in the study. It is more likely that BPE symptoms in these men resulted from smooth muscle constriction rather than from physical obstruction by excess glandular tissue. As a result, they were more likely to respond to an alpha-blocker.

A review article published in *The Journal of Urology* found that all four alpha-blockers were effective at relieving BPE symptoms. Men taking Uroxatral had a 19 to 40 percent improvement in their symptom scores; those taking Cardura had a 14 to 39 percent improvement; men who were taking Flomax had a 24 to 50 percent improvement; and those taking Hytrin had a 38 to 64 percent improvement.

Men who have both BPE and an overactive bladder (OAB) may benefit from treatment with an alpha-blocker and a drug used to treat OAB, such as tolterodine (Detrol). In one study, men who took both Flomax and Detrol experienced greater improvements in their lower urinary tract symptoms than did men taking either medication alone.

Alpha-blockers can cause side effects such as orthostatic hypotension (dizziness upon standing due to a drop in blood pressure), fatigue, insomnia and headache. These side effects are less common with Flomax because it does not lower blood pressure as much as the other alpha-blockers. Taking the drugs in the evening can minimize the risk of orthostatic hypotension.

Men who take alpha-blockers should be aware that these medications may interact with the oral phosphodiesterase type 5 (PDE5) inhibitors used to treat erectile dysfunction (ED)—sildenafil (Viagra), tadalafil (Cialis) and vardenafil (Levitra)—as the combination also can lead to hypotension.

The current recommendation is that Viagra not be taken within four hours of taking an alpha-blocker; that Levitra should not be used by anyone taking alpha-blockers; and that Cialis should be used only with Flomax at the 0.4-mg dose and not at all with the other alpha-blockers.

Among men taking blood pressure medication, alpha-blocker dosages may need to be adjusted to account for the drugs' blood pressure-lowering effects. Alpha-blockers may induce angina (chest pain resulting from an inadequate supply of oxygen to the heart) in men with coronary heart disease.

Men taking alpha-blockers who plan to undergo cataract surgery should tell their eye surgeon they are using the medication. Use of alpha-blockers has been found to make a man's iris more "floppy" during cataract surgery (a condition called floppy iris syndrome). However, the surgeon can modify the surgical technique to avoid this problem if he or she is aware of the alpha-blocker use prior to the operation (see "Ask the Doctor" at right).

JOHNS HOPKINS
MEDICINE

ASK THE DOCTOR

Q. *I have been taking tamsulosin (Flomax) for several years. I'm facing cataract surgery in the next year and I've heard that Flomax increases the risk of complications during the operation. Is this also true of the other three alpha-blocking drugs for enlarged prostate?*

A. Studies have shown that during cataract surgery, men who have been taking an alpha blocker are at increased risk for a complication known as intra-operative floppy iris syndrome (IFIS). This condition results in impaired access to the lens containing the cataract, which is located behind the iris, making surgery more difficult.

In a study in the *Journal of Cataract Refractory Surgery*, reporting on more than 1,400 patients, IFIS was rare, making up only 2 percent of all cases. Almost all the IFIS cases were in men taking tamsulosin. No patients taking other kinds of alpha blockers had this problem. Another study found that men who took tamsulosin were 2.3 times more likely to develop IFIS than men who took other alpha blockers.

The American Academy of Ophthalmology and the American Society of Cataract and Refractive Surgeons recommend informing your eye surgeon that you're using an alpha blocker for BPE, no matter which one it is. The surgeon can modify the technique and still achieve an excellent outcome.

Medications Used in the Treatment of Benign Prostatic Enlargement 2012

Drug type: Brand (generic)	Recommended daily dosage*	How to take
Alpha-1-adrenergic blockers (alpha-blockers)		
Cardura/Cardura XL (doxazosin)	1-8 mg (doctor will increase dosage slowly)	*Cardura:* 1x/day, morning or evening. *Cardura XL:* every day with breakfast. Do not chew, cut or crush tablets.
Flomax (tamsulosin)	0.4-0.8 mg	30 minutes after the same meal every day.
Hytrin (terazosin)	1-10 mg (doctor will increase dosage slowly)	Take first dose at bedtime; subsequent doses usually taken 1x/day, in the morning.
Rapaflo (silodosin)	8 mg (4 mg for men with moderate kidney disease)	Take once daily with a meal.
Uroxatral (alfuzosin)	10 mg extended release	After the same meal every day. Do not cut or crush tablets.
5-alpha-reductase inhibitors		
Avodart (dutasteride)	0.5 mg	Once daily, with or without food.
Proscar (finasteride)	5 mg	Once daily, with or without food.
Combination drug		
Jalyn (dutasteride/tamsulosin)	0.5 mg dutasteride/0.4 mg tamsulosin	30 minutes after the same meal every day.

* These dosages represent an average range for the treatment of benign prostatic hyperplasia. The precise effective dosage varies from person to person and depends on many factors. Do not make any changes in your medication without consulting your doctor.

5-alpha-reductase inhibitors

Two 5-alpha-reductase inhibitors are used to treat BPE: finasteride (Proscar) and dutasteride (Avodart). These medications inhibit the enzyme 5-alpha-reductase, which converts testosterone to dihydrotestosterone (DHT), the major male sex hormone within the cells of the prostate. Medications in this class work best in men with larger prostates—40 g (approximately 1.5 oz.) or more—whose symptoms likely

How they work	Precautions	Most common side effects	Call your doctor if...
By blocking alpha-1-adrenergic receptors, these drugs relax muscle tissue in the prostate, bladder neck and prostate capsule. The result is increased urinary flow and a reduction in urinary symptoms.	Risk of drowsiness or lightheadedness (avoid driving or operating machinery for 24 hours after the first dose or a dose increase). For Cardura and Hytrin, the initial dosage is usually 1 mg to avoid this problem. Dosage increases should be incremental. Don't take Rapaflo if you have severe kidney or liver disease. Don't take Uroxatral if you have liver problems or are taking anti-fungal drugs, protease inhibitors or another alpha-blocker for high blood pressure. If you are planning to have cataract surgery, tell your surgeon you are taking an alpha-blocker.	Dizziness (especially when standing up), headache, fatigue or sleepiness, low blood pressure, shortness of breath, nasal congestion. *Rapaflo:* Same as above and retrograde ejaculation.	You develop lightheadedness or dizziness, angina (chest or arm pain), shortness of breath, a persistent erection, a fast or irregular heartbeat, swelling in the feet or lower legs.
By blocking the enzyme 5-alpha-reductase, which converts testosterone into dihydrotestosterone (a hormone responsible for prostate growth), these drugs cause the prostate to shrink. The drugs are most effective when the prostate is significantly enlarged.	Usually requires about a year to take full effect. Most men must use indefinitely to control symptoms. Women who are pregnant or could become pregnant should not handle crushed tablets because of risk of birth defects. Do not donate blood while taking drug or for six months after stopping it to avoid passing it on to a woman or fetus.	Side effects are relatively infrequent. They include erectile dysfunction (less than 5%), decreased libido, decreased ejaculate volume, swelling of the breasts (1%).	You notice breast tenderness, enlargement or other changes; skin rash; swelling of the lips.
Same as dutasteride and tamsulosin (see above).	Same as dutasteride and tamsulosin (see above).	Same as dutasteride and tamsulosin (see above).	You have any symptoms described under dutasteride or tamsulosin (see above).

result from physical obstruction of the urethra.

The two 5-alpha-reductase inhibitors are equally effective. Both can reduce the size of the prostate by 20 to 30 percent, relieve BPE symptoms, and reduce the risk of acute urinary retention and the need for BPE surgery. However, these drugs must be continued indefinitely to prevent symptom recurrence. Moreover, it may take as long as a year to achieve maximal benefits.

Proscar and Avodart cause relatively few side effects. ED (the inability to achieve a full erection), occurs in 5 to 8 percent of men, decreased libido (sex drive) in 3 to 6 percent, reduced ejaculate in 1 percent, and breast enlargement or tenderness in 0.5 percent. Sexual side effects tend to decrease with time, and they disappear when the drug is stopped. Breast-related side effects do not diminish with time but often improve once the drug is no longer taken.

Another side effect of both Proscar and Avodart is that they lower PSA levels by about 50 percent. If not taken into account, this can interfere with the results of PSA tests to detect prostate cancer. Men should have a PSA test before starting treatment with any 5-alpha-reductase inhibitor so that subsequent PSA values can be interpreted in light of this baseline value. If a man is already taking a 5-alpha-reductase inhibitor and no baseline PSA level was obtained, the results of his current PSA test should be doubled to estimate the "true" PSA level.

A PSA level that falls less than 50 percent after a year of treatment with a 5-alpha-reductase inhibitor suggests that the drug is not being taken as directed or that prostate cancer might be present. Similarly, an increase in PSA levels while taking a 5-alpha-reductase inhibitor suggests the possibility of prostate cancer. PSA values return to their true level after the 5-alpha-reductase inhibitor is stopped.

The medication Propecia, which is a lower dose of finasteride marketed for the treatment of male pattern baldness, also lowers a man's PSA value to the same extent as Proscar. Men who use Propecia should alert their physician so their PSA results can be adjusted accordingly.

Combination therapy

The American Urological Association endorses the use of combination therapy for men with moderate to severe symptoms and clinical evidence of significant prostate enlargement. The AUA bases its recommendation on the results of several studies. The first was the MTOPS trial. The 4.5-year investigation involved more than 3,000 men who had BPE symptoms, making it the largest trial ever to compare various types of medication for the treatment of BPE. The participants were randomly assigned to one of four treatment groups: Proscar; Cardura; a combination of the two; or a placebo (inactive substance).

The researchers concluded that combination therapy is safe and appears to be more effective than either medication alone (Proscar or Cardura). Men on combination therapy were 66 percent less likely to experience worsening of their BPE during the study than were men who took the placebo. Men who took Cardura alone were 39 percent less likely to experience worsening symptoms; for those who took Proscar alone, the risk of worsening symptoms was 34 percent lower. Combination therapy also reduced the risk of acute urinary retention by 79 percent compared with placebo. The risk reduction was 67 percent with Proscar, but Cardura did not significantly affect urinary retention rates.

Other research that has shown good results from combination therapy is the Combination of Avodart and Tamsulosin (CombAT) study. In this trial, published in *BJU International*, men with BPE who were given combination therapy with the 5-alpha-reductase inhibitor Avodart and the alpha-blocker tamsulosin (Flomax) were less likely than other men who received only Flomax to experience worsening symptoms, develop acute urinary retention or need surgery. The men in this study had prostate enlargement with moderate to severe BPE symptoms. A combination drug called Jalyn (containing Avodart and Flomax) was approved recently by the Food and Drug Administration (FDA).

Combination therapy has been shown to be most effective in men with larger prostates because Proscar and Avodart work by reducing prostate size. Older men, those with higher PSA levels, and men with low urinary flow rates are more likely than other men to have an enlarged prostate.

Several potential BPE drugs are under investigation, and urologists are exploring the benefits of combining BPE medications with oral ED drugs. Treatment for one disorder often helps the other, and the combination of an oral medication for ED and an alpha-blocker works better than either agent alone for men who have both conditions. This research is expected to expand the medication options in the coming years.

Anticholinergics

Anticholinergics may be appropriate for some men with lower urinary tract symptoms. These drugs block a neurotransmitter called acetylcholine, which can act on the bladder and cause a sudden urge to urinate. Anticholinergic drugs, such as tolterodine (Detrol), are best suited for men who do not have a problem with retaining urine in the bladder and whose symptoms are primarily irritative; for example, a frequent need to urinate or sudden uncontrollable urges to urinate.

JOHNS HOPKINS
MEDICINE

LATEST RESEARCH

Finasteride for benign prostatic enlargement: Size matters

Finasteride (Proscar) is a treatment option for men with benign prostatic enlargement (BPE) and lower urinary tract symptoms. An analysis of data from the Medical Therapy of Prostatic Symptoms (MTOPS) trial suggests that Proscar is of benefit only to men with larger prostates.

In this analysis, researchers reviewed data from 1,140 men with BPE who had been randomly assigned to treatment with finasteride (5 mg) or placebo. After an average of 4.5 years, finasteride significantly reduced the rate of clinical progression of BPE—but only in men whose prostates were at least 30 mL or larger.

Initial treatment decisions for BPE are typically based on the severity of symptoms, age and overall health. But these findings suggest that prostate size should be considered as well.

THE JOURNAL OF UROLOGY
Volume 185, page 1369
April 2011

Surgery

Known as simple prostatectomy, surgery for BPE typically involves removing only the prostate tissue that is surrounding and pressing on the urethra. The procedure can be performed in one of two ways: through the urethra (transurethrally) or by making an incision in the lower abdomen.

Simple prostatectomy for BPE differs from radical prostatectomy for prostate cancer. In the cancer surgery, the surgeon removes the entire prostate and the seminal vesicles (glands located on each side of the bladder that secrete seminal fluid).

Surgery is the fastest, most reliable way to improve BPE symptoms. Fewer than 10 percent of patients will require a repeat procedure five to 10 years later. However, surgery is associated with a greater risk of long-term complications, such as ED, incontinence and retrograde ("dry") ejaculation, compared with other treatment options for BPE. (Retrograde ejaculation—ejaculation of semen into the bladder rather than through the penis—is not dangerous but can provoke anxiety and may cause infertility.) The incidence of these complications varies with the type of surgical procedure. Now that medications are available to treat BPE, fewer men are opting for surgery.

If surgery is chosen, the operation will be postponed until any urinary tract infection or kidney damage from urinary retention has been successfully treated. Because blood loss can be a complication during and immediately following most types of BPE surgery, men taking aspirin should stop taking it seven to 10 days prior to surgery. Aspirin interferes with blood clotting.

Transurethral prostatectomy

Also called transurethral resection of the prostate (TURP), this procedure is considered the gold standard for BPE treatment—the one against which other therapies are compared. More than 90 percent of simple prostatectomies for BPE are performed transurethrally. The procedure is typically done in the hospital under general or spinal anesthesia. In men with smaller prostates and no other medical problems, TURP may be performed as an outpatient procedure.

In TURP, prostate tissue is removed with a resectoscope, a long, thin instrument that is inserted into the penis and passed through the urethra to the prostate. The resectoscope has a wire loop at the end to cut away prostate tissue piece by piece and to seal blood vessels with an electric current or laser energy. As the pieces of tissue are being cut away, they are washed into the bladder and then flushed out of the body through the resectoscope. A sample of the

tissue is examined in the pathology laboratory to rule out the presence of prostate cancer.

Once the surgery is completed, a catheter is inserted through the urethra into the bladder. Fluid is continuously circulated to prevent blood clot formation and to monitor for bleeding. The catheter typically remains in place for one to three days. (It may be removed in the hospital, or a man may go home with the catheter and then return a few days later to have it removed.) Most men experience a greater urgency to urinate for approximately 12 to 24 hours after the catheter is taken out. A hospital stay of one or two days is common with TURP. Men typically experience little or no pain after the procedure, and a full recovery can be expected within three weeks.

Improvement in symptoms is noticeable almost immediately after surgery and is greatest in men who had the worst symptoms beforehand. Marked improvement occurs in about 90 to 95 percent of men with severe symptoms and in about 80 percent of those with moderate symptoms. This rate of improvement is significantly better than that which can be achieved with medication or through the self-help measures employed during watchful waiting. In addition, more than 95 percent of men who undergo TURP require no further treatment over the next five years.

The most common complications immediately following TURP are bleeding, urinary tract infection and urinary retention. Longer-term complications can include ED, retrograde ejaculation and incontinence, all of which can be treated. However, increasing evidence suggests that TURP may cause no more problems with sexual function than other treatments for BPE and, in some instances, may even bring about improvements in sexual functioning. The risk of death from TURP is very low (0.1 percent).

Open prostatectomy

An open prostatectomy is the surgery most often performed when a man's prostate is so large that TURP can't be performed safely. Two types of open prostatectomy can be performed for BPE: suprapubic and retropubic. Both require an incision from between the navel and the pubic bone.

A suprapubic prostatectomy involves opening the bladder and removing the inner portion of the prostate through the bladder. In a retropubic procedure the bladder is moved aside and the inner prostate tissue is removed without entering the bladder. Both procedures are performed in a hospital under general or spinal anesthesia. As in TURP, removed tissue is checked for prostate cancer.

Sacral Nerve Stimulation for Lower Urinary Tract Symptoms

Answers to eight common questions

If you have an overactive bladder along with urinary symptoms such as leaking, urgency and frequency, lifestyle changes, behavioral modification or medication—alone or in combination—are the treatments of choice. But, according to American Urological Association guidelines, when those measures don't work and symptoms are severe, sacral neuromodulation is a reasonable option to consider. If you're not familiar with this technology, here are answers to some questions you may have.

1. How does sacral neuromodulation work?

The bladder and muscles that relate to urination are controlled by a series of chemical and electrical "messages" exchanged between the brain and a group of nerves at the base of the spine called the sacral nerve plexus.

Sometimes a malfunction in the "electrical system" causes the delivery of faulty messages regarding what the bladder and the nerves that control it should—or should not—do, and this can lead to problems controlling your bladder.

With sacral neuromodulation, a small thin electrical device known as a neurostimulator is used to send electrical pulses to a sacral nerve.

In some people, these mild shocks correct the faulty electrical messages that trigger the brain to think the bladder needs to empty when it really doesn't or shouldn't.

The device, marketed as the InterStim System, has been approved by the Food and Drug Administration (FDA) since 1997. However, only recently has it been recommended for consideration as a potential treatment for men with benign prostatic enlargement (BPE) who are appropriate candidates.

2. Is it painful?

Your doctor will determine the initial settings for the device. Although the intensity of the electrical stimulation varies from person to person, it should not be painful. Most people describe the sensation as a slight "pulling" or "tingling" in the pelvic area. If the intensity is too strong or too weak, you can adjust it with a hand-held controller.

3. Does it work for everyone?

Unfortunately, no. To determine whether neuromodulation will work for you, you'll need to wear a temporary external device for a brief trial period. To place the device during the trial, your doctor will numb a small area in your lower back. Next, the doctor will temporarily implant one end of a thin, flexible wire, or lead, near

After a suprapubic prostatectomy, two catheters are placed in the bladder, one through the urethra and the other through an opening made in the lower abdominal wall. The catheters remain in place for three to seven days after surgery. Following a retropubic prostatectomy, a catheter is placed in the bladder through the urethra and remains in place for a week. The hospital stay (two to three days) and the recovery period (four to six weeks) are longer for open prostatectomy than for TURP.

Like TURP, an open prostatectomy is an effective way to relieve symptoms of BPE. However, complications are more common with open prostatectomy—and in some cases the complications can be life threatening. As a result, open prostatectomy is reserved for otherwise healthy men with the largest prostates. The most common complications immediately after open prostatectomy are wound your tailbone. The remaining portion of the lead is then taped to your skin and connected to an external device that you wear on your waistband. After the temporary device is turned on, it sends electrical pulses through the lead to your sacral nerves. You'll know that the therapy is working if you notice significant improvement in your symptoms.

Based on the outcome of the trial, you and your doctor can decide on the next step, including whether to go ahead with long-term implantation.

4. What does long-term implantation involve?

Following a successful trial, the temporary lead will be removed and a long-term lead and a small thin neurostimulator will be surgically implanted just under the skin in your upper buttock.

This minimally invasive procedure can be performed as an outpatient surgery while you are under local anesthesia. The device can be turned off or removed at any time.

5. Are there risks?

Implanting an InterStim System has risks similar to those seen with any surgical procedure, including swelling, bruising, bleeding and infection. In addition to risks related to surgery, other complications can occur. These may include pain at the implant sites, new pain, infection, movement of the wire, device problems, undesirable changes in urinary function or uncomfortable stimulation (sometimes described as a jolting or shocking feeling), or interactions with other electrical devices, such as pacemakers or diagnostic equipment.

6. Can I perform my normal activities?

Because the temporary wire can move, you'll be advised to avoid bending, stretching or lifting heavy objects during the trial period. Once implanted for long-term use and after your surgical incisions have healed, it will not impair your ability to perform your normal activities.

7. How long does it last?

The InterStim neurostimulator has a battery life of five years, but your doctor can estimate how long it's likely to last after it has been implanted. The more stimulation you need, the faster your battery will drain. When the battery runs out, the entire neurostimulator will need to be replaced because the battery is encased in the device.

8. Is the cost covered by health insurance?

Yes. Medicare and many private insurers cover this treatment. ■

infection and excessive bleeding, which may require a transfusion.

More serious complications of an open prostatectomy, although rare, include heart attack, pneumonia and pulmonary embolism (a blood clot that travels to the lungs). Performing breathing exercises, moving the legs in bed and walking soon after surgery can reduce the risk of pneumonia and blood clots. Long-term complications, including ED, incontinence and retrograde ejaculation, are slightly more common with open prostatectomy than with TURP.

Alternative Surgical Approaches

Transurethral electrovaporization

Also known as TUVP, this procedure is a modification of TURP. As in TURP, the procedure involves inserting a resectoscope through the urethra. But instead of a wire loop to cut away the tissue, the resectoscope has a grooved roller at the end, through which a powerful electric current is delivered to vaporize prostate tissue with minimal bleeding. A catheter is placed in the bladder after the procedure.

In a meta-analysis of 20 randomized, controlled trials, investigators compared TURP with TUVP. They found no differences in urinary symptom scores or peak urinary flow rates after one year.

However, TUVP was associated with less need for transfusion, a shorter catheterization time and a shorter hospital stay when compared with TURP. On the other hand, TURP was associated with a lower risk of urinary retention after surgery and a lower risk of needing a reoperation when compared with TUVP.

Transurethral incision of the prostate

Like TURP, transurethral incision of the prostate (TUIP) is performed with a resectoscope inserted through the urethra. However, instead of cutting away prostate tissue, the surgeon makes one or two small incisions in the prostate with an electrical knife or laser. These incisions alleviate the symptoms of BPE by decreasing the pressure that excess prostate tissue exerts on the urethra. A tissue sample is often obtained to check for prostate cancer.

TUIP takes less time to perform than TURP and, in most cases, can be done on an outpatient basis under general or spinal anesthesia.

TUIP is effective only in men with prostates smaller than 30 g (about 1 oz.). The degree of symptom improvement in these men is similar to that achieved with TURP, but patients may be more likely to require a second procedure. Because the incidence of retrograde ejaculation is lower than with TURP, TUIP is a good option for men concerned about their fertility.

Holmium laser prostatectomy

The holmium laser can used in a variety of ways to treat BPE. In Holmium laser ablation of the prostate (HOLAP), the excess prostate tissue is destroyed by the laser. Results appear similar to those achieved with TURP and open prostatectomy. The main advantages of HOLAP appear to be reduced blood loss and shorter catheterization times and hospital stays.

A variation of HOLAP is Holmium laser resection of the prostate (HoLRP). In this procedure, a Holmium laser is used to cut the excess tissue.

Another option is Holmium laser enucleation of the prostate (HOLEP). This is a relatively new procedure for the transurethral

removal of a prostate weighing more than 100 g (about 3.5 oz.).

Like TURP, Holmium laser prostatectomy has the potential to cause ED and retrograde ejaculation.

Photoselective vaporization of the prostate

Also called Green Light laser vaporization, photoselective vaporization of the prostate (PVP) uses a wavelength that is highly absorbed by hemoglobin. This results in minimal blood loss during the procedure. PVP allows tissue removal similar to the traditional TURP procedure while maintaining the safety characteristics of lasers.

Minimally Invasive Therapy

The goal of minimally invasive treatment for BPE is to reduce lower urinary tract symptoms and thereby improve quality of life, while minimizing treatment side effects. A variety of minimally invasive procedures have been introduced as alternatives to TURP. These therapies use heat to vaporize tissue in the prostate, a process known as thermoablation. How thermoablation works is not entirely clear. It may improve symptoms by reducing smooth muscle tone within the prostate or by simply destroying prostate tissue.

The advantages of minimally invasive therapies over TURP are that they are performed on an outpatient basis and are associated with fewer adverse events, such as bleeding, incontinence and retrograde ejaculation. However, minimally invasive procedures also have a number of disadvantages. First, it takes longer for symptoms to improve with these therapies. Second, the risk of urinary retention is as high as 40 percent. Third, more than half of men need further treatment at some point. Fourth, no tissue sample is available to test for prostate cancer. Finally, the long-term effectiveness of these treatments is not as well established when compared with TURP.

Although there are a number of minimally invasive therapies for BPE, the most commonly used are transurethral microwave thermotherapy (TUMT) and transurethral needle ablation (TUNA).

Transurethral microwave thermotherapy

In TUMT, a catheter inserted through the urethra delivers microwave energy that heats prostate tissue to temperatures above 113° F, causing death (coagulative necrosis) of prostate tissue. At the same time, a cooling system prevents damage to the surrounding tissue, particularly the urethra. This procedure requires only a local anesthetic, which is placed within the urethra.

TUMT is most appropriate for men who have moderately sized

prostates (30 to 60 g, approximately 1 to 2 oz.) and symptoms that are moderate to severe (International Prostate Symptom Score of 8 or higher). Research shows that TUMT typically results in a 40 to 70 percent reduction in symptom scores.

In a five-year study comparing TUMT and TURP, researchers found no significant differences between the two techniques regarding improvements in symptoms, quality of life, peak urinary flow rate or residual urine volume. However, more men treated with TUMT required additional treatment after several years—10 percent versus 4 percent of those who underwent TURP.

Side effects from TUMT are usually minor and generally disappear with time. TUMT is less likely than TURP to cause bleeding or sexual dysfunction, but it is associated with a higher risk of urinary tract infection. These infections usually result from catheterization, and the longer the catheter is in place, the higher the risk. Men undergoing TUMT usually have a catheter in place for two to 14 days. Antibiotics are often prescribed either after the procedure or after catheter removal to reduce the risk of infection. Other side effects of TUMT include short-term incontinence and urinary retention.

Transurethral needle ablation

With TUNA, tiny needles are advanced through the urethra to deliver radiofrequency energy to the prostate tissue. Men with larger prostates may require several needle punctures.

One advantage of this approach is that the surgeon can target specific areas of the prostate; other minimally invasive therapies deliver heat to the entire gland. However, TUNA usually requires intravenous sedation in addition to local anesthesia.

In a randomized trial reported in *The Journal of Urology*, investigators compared TUNA with TURP. They found that the treatment benefits of both procedures were maintained at five years. TUNA, however, was associated with fewer complications. For example, ED occurred in 3 percent of TUNA patients compared with 21 percent of TURP patients. In addition, none of the TUNA patients experienced retrograde ejaculation compared with 41 percent of the men who underwent TURP. Furthermore, TUNA patients were less likely to experience incontinence or to develop urethral strictures. Since the publication of this study in 2004, however, relatively little additional research on TUNA for the treatment of BPE has been performed. And, according to the AUA, while TUNA appears to be safe, the lack of high-quality studies leaves a "degree of uncertainty" about the procedure's benefits.

PROSTATE CANCER

Autopsy studies have shown microscopic evidence of prostate cancer in 15 to 30 percent of men over the age of 50 and in 60 to 70 percent of men who reach age 80. These numbers have led some experts to theorize that every man will develop some degree of prostate cancer if he lives long enough.

Although the number of men diagnosed with prostate cancer has increased with the widespread use of the prostate-specific antigen (PSA) blood test for screening, prostate cancer death rates began to decline after 1993 and have fallen by 40 percent. Many experts believe that earlier detection of prostate cancer through routine use of the PSA test was responsible for the declining death rates. This has been a matter of great debate (see "Should You Have a PSA Screening Test?" on page 33).

A boy born today has a 16 percent chance of being diagnosed with prostate cancer at some time in his life and a 3 percent chance of dying of the disease. The good news is that statistics from a large national health database indicate that the vast majority of men diagnosed with prostate cancer will live as long as men in the same age group who never develop the disease.

Risk Factors for Prostate Cancer

The underlying cause of prostate cancer is unknown. As with other cancers, however, multiple events over a period of many years are probably necessary to produce a cancerous change in a prostate cell. The development of cancer is broadly viewed as a two-step process. In the first step, cancer is initiated through genetic alterations in the cell. This is followed by cancer promotion, a process that allows the cancerous cells to continue to grow and progress. The study of factors that initiate and promote prostate cancer is an active area of investigation.

Age, race and family history are all important risk factors for prostate cancer. In addition, diet and lifestyle factors may influence whether a man will develop the disease. Studies have shown no clear association between the development of prostate cancer and regular alcohol intake (though binge drinking may increase the risk), smoking, vasectomy or the presence of benign prostatic enlargement, or BPE, also known as benign prostatic hyperplasia (BPH).

Increasing evidence suggests that fat intake, physical inactivity or

LATEST RESEARCH

Startling findings on smoking and prostate cancer

Need another reason to quit smoking? A recent study suggests that smoking at the time of prostate cancer diagnosis is associated with an increased risk of biochemical recurrence and an increased risk of dying from prostate cancer as well. This is the first large-scale study to demonstrate that smoking increases the risk of dying from prostate cancer.

Researchers followed 5,366 men diagnosed with prostate cancer over two decades. Of these, 1,630 died—524 due to prostate cancer and 416 due to cardiovascular disease—and 878 had recurrences of their prostate cancer after treatment.

When compared with men who had never smoked, those who were smoking at the time of diagnosis had an approximately 60 percent greater risk of prostate cancer recurrence after treatment and death from prostate cancer. Furthermore, the greater the number of years spent smoking, the greater the risk of death due to prostate cancer.

There was some good news—and inspiration to stop smoking: Men who had quit smoking for 10 or more years had prostate-related death and recurrence rates that were similar to those of nonsmokers.

JAMA
Volume 305, page 2548
June 22/29, 2011

being overweight may influence the development or progression of prostate cancer. Whether testosterone replacement therapy affects the development or progression of prostate cancer is not clear. If prostate cancer is present, however, it is believed to cause the disease to progress more rapidly in some men.

Age

As a man ages, his risk of developing prostate cancer increases dramatically. This age-related increase is greater for prostate cancer than for any other type of cancer. The average age at diagnosis is between 65 and 70; the average age at death is 80.

Race

The incidence (new cases per 100,000 men per year) of prostate cancer in the United States varies by race. Black men are at highest risk, with a rate of 234 per 100,000 men each year. The rate for white men is 150 per 100,000. Asian American men have a lower risk, 88 per 100,000.

Family History

Studies of identical and fraternal twins have found that prostate cancer has a stronger hereditary component than many other cancers, including breast and colon cancer. Having one first-degree relative (a brother or father) with prostate cancer doubles the risk of developing the disease; having a second-degree relative (an uncle or grandfather) with the disease confers only a small increase in risk.

A number of genetic alterations that affect how the body handles inflammation and infections, fat metabolism, repair of genetic damage and other processes have been linked to prostate cancer development and progression. For example, researchers have discovered that gene fusions—a process in which genes separate from their normal location and fuse to another gene—are an early event in prostate cancer development.

Rather than inheriting a defect in a single gene that results in prostate cancer, it is more likely that minor variations in a number of genes (any one of which alone may have no adverse effects) when combined may act like the "perfect storm" to increase a man's risk. The lifestyle choices a man makes during life most likely act in concert with these genetic variants to cause the development and progression of prostate cancer.

Although genes can influence a man's risk of developing prostate cancer, other factors also are at work. The likelihood that identical

twins (who share all genetic information) will both develop prostate cancer is 27 percent. This suggests that lifestyle choices can modify the effects of the genetic cards that a person is dealt at birth.

Lifestyle Factors

Much effort has been devoted to searching for lifestyle or environmental factors that might serve as promoters for prostate cancer. The incidence of microscopic prostate cancer (cancers too small to be seen except under a microscope) is similar among men in the United States and in all other countries that have been examined. However, the death rates from prostate cancer differ from one country to another and even within different regions of the United States. These differences suggest that factors such as diet, exercise, body weight or exposure to certain substances or forces influence prostate cancer's progression from microscopic tumors to clinically significant ones.

Some factors are believed to encourage the growth of prostate cancer, whereas others may have a protective effect. It is important to remember, however, that the effects of diet and lifestyle are difficult to study and that research results are often conflicting. Some researchers believe that an individual's overall dietary pattern—following a primarily plant-based diet, for instance—may be more important than individual foods and nutrients.

Dietary fat

Many studies that have looked at the relationship between dietary fat and prostate cancer have found a higher risk of the disease among men with a higher fat intake (especially saturated fat from animal products). Fat makes up 30 to 40 percent of the calories in the American diet, compared with 15 percent in Japan. This difference in fat consumption may help explain the much lower death rate from prostate cancer in Japan as well as the great variability in prostate cancer mortality rates around the world. It is also possible that people who consume large amounts of high-fat foods are less likely to eat healthful foods, such as fruits and vegetables, which may protect against cancer.

Omega-3 fatty acids, which have anti-inflammatory and anti-cancer effects, are an important exception. These "good fats" are abundant in fatty fish like salmon, sardines, tuna and halibut and in fish oil. Several studies suggest that men who eat fish two or more times per week have a reduced risk of developing prostate cancer. Flaxseed, walnuts and canola oil contain a weaker but still beneficial form of these healthy fats.

Vegetables and fruits

A high intake of vegetables may lower the risk of prostate cancer. In a study in the *Journal of the National Cancer Institute*, men who ate 28 or more servings of vegetables a week (four a day) were 35 percent less likely to develop prostate cancer than those who ate 14 or fewer servings per week (two a day). Men who ate cruciferous vegetables, such as cabbage and broccoli, appeared to be at even lower risk: Those who ate three or more servings of cruciferous vegetables a week (in addition to other vegetables) had a 41 percent lower risk of prostate cancer than those who ate less than one serving a week. Cruciferous vegetables are rich in substances that help detoxify cancer-causing substances (carcinogens).

Regular consumption of soy foods (such as tofu, soy protein and soy milk) has been linked to a reduced risk of developing prostate cancer.

Lycopene-rich cooked tomato products (for example, tomato paste, spaghetti sauce and ketchup) also may be protective, although this is controversial. (Lycopene is an antioxidant, a substance that detoxifies damaging molecules called free radicals.) For example, in the Physicians' Health Study, men who consumed the most tomato products had a lower risk of prostate cancer than those who consumed the least. In addition, pomegranates and pomegranate juice (which have strong anti-inflammatory and antioxidant effects) are under investigation for their potential to slow the progression of prostate cancer.

Vitamins and minerals

Both vitamin E and the mineral selenium have long been under study for their potential to prevent or slow the progression of prostate cancer. In one early study, men who took vitamin E supplements had a 34 percent reduction in the incidence of prostate cancer. Another study found that men who took selenium supplements had a two-thirds reduction in the risk of developing prostate cancer.

In late 2008, however, long-awaited results from a large, nationwide clinical trial called SELECT (Selenium and Vitamin E for the Prevention of Prostate Cancer) found that men who took vitamin E, selenium or both developed prostate cancer as often as men who did not take them. More recent findings from the SELECT trial, published in 2010 in the *Journal of the American Medical Association*, found that men who consumed 400 IU of vitamin E per day for seven years were more likely to develop prostate cancer than men who took a placebo.

In recent years, a high intake of calcium has come under scrutiny as a possible risk factor for prostate cancer. In one study, the risk of developing advanced prostate cancer was 2.5 times higher among men who consumed 2,000 mg or more of calcium each day than among men with a daily consumption of 500 to 749 mg. For now, a sensible approach is to limit calcium consumption to no more than 1,200 mg per day through food sources.

Energy balance

The relationship between calories taken in versus calories burned—energy balance—also may affect prostate cancer risk. Animal research has shown that implanted cancers grow more slowly when the animals' calorie intake is restricted. Preliminary evidence suggests that men with the greatest calorie intake are more likely to develop prostate cancer than are those whose consumption is more modest.

In one study, men who consumed the most calories (approximately 2,600 per day) were nearly four times as likely to have prostate cancer as men who consumed the least (1,100 per day). Nonetheless, more research is needed before recommendations regarding calorie intake can be made.

Regular vigorous physical activity helps improve energy balance by burning calories, and increasing research suggests that exercise offers a protective effect against prostate cancer. Results from the Health Professionals Follow-up Study indicate that men age 65 or older who are vigorous exercisers are 70 percent less likely to develop life-threatening prostate cancer.

Excess weight

Obesity—defined as having a body mass index (BMI) of 30 or more—is known to increase the risk of some types of cancer as well as cancer deaths. It is unclear whether obesity influences the development of prostate cancer specifically; however, several studies have found that obese men have higher-grade prostate cancers at diagnosis and a higher risk of cancer recurrence after radical prostatectomy and radiation treatment than men who are not obese. Researchers hypothesize that obesity may contribute to cancer progression by altering blood levels of sex hormones or insulin.

Sunlight exposure and vitamin D

Sunlight may protect against prostate cancer by promoting the body's production of vitamin D. Vitamin D is produced in the skin during exposure to the ultraviolet (UV) radiation in sunlight.

LATEST RESEARCH

Coffee drinking linked to reduced risk of aggressive prostate cancer

Men who drink at least six cups of coffee a day may be reducing their risk of advanced prostate cancer, new research suggests.

In this observational study, researchers reviewed data on nearly 48,000 men who took part in the Health Professionals Follow-Up Study and reported their consumption of regular and decaffeinated coffee in 1986 and every four years thereafter until 2006. During that period, there were 5,035 cases of prostate cancer, including 642 that were lethal, defined as metastatic or fatal.

The investigators found that drinking six or more cups of coffee each day was associated with an 18 percent lower risk of developing prostate cancer, compared with no coffee drinking. In addition, the coffee drinkers' odds of developing lethal prostate cancer were 60 percent lower. Even men who drank only one to three cups a day had a 30 percent lower risk of developing lethal prostate cancer. The reductions in risk were observed for both caffeinated or decaffeinated coffee.

There's probably no harm in drinking a few cups of coffee every day if you enjoy it, but based on the findings from a single observational study, it's too early to recommend it to reduce the risk of prostate cancer—lethal or otherwise.

JOURNAL OF THE NATIONAL CANCER INSTITUTE
Volume 103, page 876
June 8, 2011

Prevention of Prostate Cancer

Finasteride (Proscar), which is used to treat BPE, has been studied as a potential preventive agent in prostate cancer. In the landmark Prostate Cancer Prevention Trial (PCPT), investigators reported a lower incidence of prostate cancer among Proscar users; 18 percent of the men taking Proscar were diagnosed with prostate cancer, compared with 24 percent of men taking a placebo. A more recent study found that another BPE drug, dutasteride (Avodart), produced similar results.

However, it is not known if these medications, which belong to a class of drugs known as 5-alpha reductase inhibitors, actually prevent prostate cancer or if they simply lower PSA levels. In the trials studying finasteride and dutasteride for prostate cancer prevention, men taking the drugs were less likely to undergo a prostate biopsy because their PSA levels were lower. Thus, 5-alpha reductase inhibitors may just prevent a man from knowing that he has the disease.

The development of aggressive tumors (Gleason score of 7 to 10) has been another concern for men taking 5-alpha reductase inhibitors. Aggressive tumors were diagnosed twice as often among men taking these medications, a finding that prompted the Food and Drug Administration (FDA) to conclude that Proscar and Avodart should not be used for prostate cancer prevention.

Other drugs have also been investigated for prostate cancer prevention but none has proven to be effective.

Symptoms of Prostate Cancer

Prostate cancer typically causes no symptoms in its early stages. In men with advanced disease, however, urinary symptoms may occur. These symptoms are indistinguishable from those of BPE except that they may appear more abruptly when due to cancer.

A man with prostate cancer may experience erectile dysfunction (ED) or a decrease in the firmness of erections if the cancer has invaded the nerves beside the prostate that control erections. In some men the first symptoms of prostate cancer originate in areas of the body where the cancer has spread (severe back pain from cancer that has spread to the spine, for example).

Today, the diagnosis of prostate cancer at these advanced stages is unusual because of widespread screening for the disease with the PSA test.

Diagnosis of Prostate Cancer

The diagnosis of prostate cancer typically begins with an abnormal PSA test result or perhaps a worrisome finding on a digital rectal exam (DRE). If either the PSA test or digital rectal exam suggests cancer, either a transrectal ultrasound or a prostate biopsy will be performed.

Digital Rectal Examination

Diagnosing prostate cancer at an early stage can be difficult with DRE alone because the cancer cells tend to spread throughout the prostate instead of forming a solid mass that can be easily felt. Used alone, digital rectal exams miss approximately 30 to 40 percent of prostate cancers, and most cancers found with the exam are in a later, less treatable stage. The most reliable way to detect prostate cancer in its early stages is to combine digital rectal exams with PSA testing.

Prostate-Specific Antigen Test

The prostate-specific antigen (PSA) test measures an enzyme produced almost exclusively by the glandular cells of the prostate. It is secreted during ejaculation into the prostatic ducts that empty into the urethra.

PSA liquefies semen after ejaculation, promoting the release of sperm. Normally, only very small amounts of PSA are present in the blood. But an abnormality of the prostate can disrupt the normal architecture of the gland and create an opening for PSA to pass into the bloodstream. Thus, high blood levels of PSA can indicate prostate problems, including cancer. PSA blood levels are expressed as nanograms per milliliter (ng/mL).

A blood test to measure levels of PSA was first approved by the FDA in 1986 as a way to determine whether prostate cancer had been treated successfully and to monitor for its recurrence. Today, PSA tests are approved for prostate cancer detection and are widely used to screen men for the disease.

Clinical studies, including a randomized trial known as the European Study of Screening for Prostate Cancer (ESRPC), have shown that PSA testing saves lives by detecting and treating prostate cancer earlier. In the most recent results from this trial, prostate cancer deaths were reduced by about 40 percent among men who were screened with the PSA test compared with those who were not screened. This reduction in prostate cancer deaths is similar to the decline in prostate cancer deaths seen in the United States since the onset of widespread PSA testing in the late 1980s.

Clinical studies to date have demonstrated the following benefits of PSA testing: (1) An elevated PSA is the single best predictor of the presence of prostate cancer; (2) PSA testing detects prostate cancer about five to 10 years earlier than digital rectal exams; (3) Most cancers detected with PSA testing are curable; (4) Regularly scheduled PSA testing virtually eliminates the diagnosis of advanced prostate cancer; and (5) A baseline PSA test in midlife (age 40s or 50s) can help predict the risk of prostate cancer up to 25 years later.

Because some of the cancers detected by PSA screening are so small or slow growing that they might never have become life threatening, the trade off of routine screening is the overdiagnosis of non-life-threatening cancers for which treatment is not necessary. This occurs more often in older men, who have less to gain from screening because of a shorter life expectancy.

Another drawback of PSA testing is that most men with an elevated PSA do not have prostate cancer. Instead, prostate enlargement (BPE) or inflammation is to blame. These men may undergo unnecessary diagnostic tests and treatments and may experience undue anxiety. Because of these uncertainties, men should discuss both the benefits and limitations of PSA testing with their physician before having their PSA levels measured.

In the U.S., however, most men choose to be screened. A recent recommendation from the U.S. Preventive Services Task Force (USP-STF) may alter that practice (see "Should You Have a PSA Screening Test?" on page 33).

The likelihood of having prostate cancer varies by PSA level and whether or not the DRE is normal. The risk increases incrementally as PSA rises and, within any given PSA range, is higher if the DRE is abnormal. The risks of finding prostate cancer on a biopsy in men who have a normal DRE are as follows: a PSA of 0 to 2 ng/mL translates to a risk of 12 percent; 2 to 4 ng/mL, a 15 to 25 percent risk; 4 to 10 ng/mL, a 17 to 32 percent risk; 10 to 20 ng/mL, a 50 to 75 percent risk; and a PSA higher than 20 ng/mL, a 90 percent risk.

A study based on data from the National Institute on Aging found that a PSA level above the median value for age (0.6 ng/mL for men age 40 to 49; 0.7 ng/mL for men age 50 to 59) was associated with a three- to fourfold greater risk of prostate cancer up to 25 years later when compared with a value below the median. Swedish researchers showed that men with a PSA of 0.51 to 1.0 ng/mL or 1.01 to 2 ng/mL before age 50 had a twofold and sevenfold greater risk, respectively, of advanced prostate cancer up to 25 years later than men whose PSA level was 0.5 ng/mL or below before age 50.

Should You Have a PSA Screening Test?

Controversial recommendation says it's unnecessary in healthy men

By now, you've probably heard that prostate-specific antigen (PSA) screening is no longer recommended for healthy men under age 75. This controversial draft recommendation was issued late in 2011 by the United States Preventive Services Task Force (USPSTF).

Given previous recommendations from the medical community encouraging screening, many men are confused. Following are answers to some important questions you may have about this recommendation—and our advice on whether you should follow it.

What is the USPSTF? The USPSTF is an independent group of 16 medical experts whose recommendations serve as guidelines for doctors throughout the country. In addition, the group's recommendations ultimately impact what tests Medicare and private insurers will pay for.

Why did they make this recommendation? According to the USPSTF, the potential harms caused by PSA testing of healthy men to identify prostate cancer far outweigh its potential to save lives. The Task Force discourages the use of any screening test for which the benefits do not

outweigh the harms to the target population.

What are the potential harms of PSA screening? An elevated reading can lead to an unnecessary prostate biopsy. Although biopsies often reveal signs of cancer, depending on a man's age, 30 to 50 percent will not be harmful—even if left untreated.

After a positive biopsy comes the decision about what to do. Most men choose radical prostatectomy, external-beam radiation therapy or brachytherapy. But each of these treatments has the potential to cause serious adverse effect like erectile dysfunction, urinary incontinence or bowel damage. And men who choose active surveillance must live with the uncertainty of knowing that they have an untreated cancer that could start to progress at any time.

Why do they believe PSA screening does not save lives? The USPSTF evaluated data from five large randomized clinical trials of PSA testing, including the Prostate, Lung, Colorectal, and Ovarian Cancer (PLCO) Trial, which reported no mortality benefit among 77,000 men who underwent PSA testing and were followed for ten years.

Do these recommendations apply to all men? Yes. They apply to all men regardless of age, race or family history as long as they do not have symptoms of prostate cancer.

Our advice. Many leading cancer and patient groups and doctors, including the author of this White Paper, agree that there is harm with PSA screening and the treatment that follows diagnosis. But a more targeted screening approach focusing on those at greatest risk of developing prostate cancer, and active surveillance for those who don't need immediate treatment, could shift the balance of benefit and harm towards benefit.

PSA screening is the best test available for the detection of cancer cells in the prostate. Rather than discontinuing use of the only test available to detect the disease early and treat it successfully, efforts should focus on reducing harm.

Therefore, every man should discuss the benefits and risks of PSA screening with his physician. If you choose to be screened and the result is positive, you and your doctor should discuss whether any further intervention is appropriate or necessary. ∎

Experts now believe that this information can be used to recommend less frequent screening for men with very low PSA levels.

There is no PSA level below which physicians can reassure a man that he does not have prostate cancer. Therefore, it is not possible to define a "normal" level. In men in their 40s or men without prostate enlargement, PSA levels above 2 to 2.5 ng/mL can signal trouble, especially if rising. For older men, levels above 3 to 4 ng/mL usually indicate the need for a prostate biopsy. Most experts agree that PSA should be used in conjunction with other information (for example, family history, race and age) to assess the overall likelihood that prostate cancer is present following a discussion with the patient about the benefits and risks.

The American Cancer Society recommends that PSA testing and DRE be offered beginning at age 50. Men at increased risk for prostate cancer—black men and men with a family history of prostate cancer—should be offered PSA and DRE beginning at age 40 or 45. The American Urological Association recommends that all men consider having a baseline PSA test at age 40.

Previously, both organizations recommended annual testing for men who chose to be screened. However the American Cancer Society now recommends screening every two years for men with a PSA level below 2.5 ng/mL.

The USPSTF recommends that men age 75 and older not undergo screening for prostate cancer and contends that the current evidence is insufficient to assess the balance of benefits and harms of prostate cancer screening in men younger than age 75. In 2011, the USPSTF broadened that recommendation to include younger men as well. In spite of the USPSTF position, many experts feel that PSA screening is of value (see "Should You Have a PSA Screening Test?" on page 33). The American Urological Association and other organizations may clarify their current guidelines in response to the Task Force's latest recommendations.

A study by the Medical Editor of this White Paper found that testing all men at age 40, age 45, and then every other year after age 50 might be a better strategy, saving more lives and being less expensive than other screening schedules. Other studies have concluded that men age 50 and older who have PSA levels below 2 ng/mL do not need to be tested every year. However, the testing schedule should be more frequent if a man's PSA is rising but has not reached a threshold level where a biopsy would be recommended.

Several factors may affect the results of a PSA test. For example, some studies show that ejaculation one or two days before a PSA test may increase PSA levels in the blood. Consequently, men should abstain from sex for 72 hours prior to a PSA test.

Digital rectal exams and biopsies of the prostate may also affect PSA levels, although the increase in PSA caused by a digital rectal exam is not believed to be significant enough to produce a false-positive test result in most men. A prostate biopsy, however, may elevate PSA levels for four weeks or longer.

Other prostate problems (such as BPE or prostatitis) also can inflate PSA levels, and 5-alpha-reductase inhibitors for BPE treatment (Proscar and Avodart) can lower PSA levels by about 50 percent. When men who are taking a 5-alpha-reductase inhibitor have a PSA test, this drug-related reduction in PSA level must be taken into account to avoid misinterpretation of the test result.

Researchers have developed several ways to improve the PSA test's accuracy. These improvements include assessing PSA level in relation to prostate size (PSA density); monitoring annual changes in PSA (PSA velocity); measuring the ratio of free to total PSA (percent free PSA); and adjusting the PSA result for a patient's age (age-specific PSA). None of these take the place of a simple PSA measurement for screening.

PSA density

This measurement takes the size of a man's prostate into account when evaluating his PSA level. It is calculated by dividing the PSA value by the size of the prostate (as determined by transrectal ultrasound; see page 38). This measurement helps doctors distinguish between BPE and prostate cancer.

The higher the PSA density, the greater the chance of cancer, because the elevated PSA level is less likely to be the result of benign prostate enlargement. Several studies have found that a PSA density greater than 0.15 indicates a higher risk of cancer. PSA density appears most useful in diagnosing prostate cancer in men with PSA levels between 4 ng/mL and 10 ng/mL.

PSA velocity

This measurement takes into account annual changes in PSA values, which rise more rapidly in men with prostate cancer than in men without the disease. A study from Johns Hopkins and the National Institute on Aging found that an increase in PSA level of more than 0.75 ng/mL per year was an early predictor of prostate cancer in men with PSA levels between 4 ng/mL and 10 ng/mL.

PSA velocity is especially helpful in detecting early cancer in men with mildly elevated PSA levels and a normal digital rectal exam. It is most useful in predicting the presence of cancer when changes in PSA are evaluated over at least one to two years. In a study reported in the *New England Journal of Medicine*, a rapid rise in PSA level (more than 2 ng/mL) in the year before prostate cancer diagnosis and surgical treatment predicted a higher likelihood that a man would die of his cancer over the next seven years.

Moreover, a Johns Hopkins study published in the *Journal of the National Cancer Institute* found that a man's PSA velocity 10 to 15 years before he was diagnosed with prostate cancer predicted his survival from the disease 25 years later. In the study, 92 percent of men with an earlier PSA velocity of 0.35 ng/mL or less per year had survived, compared with 54 percent of men whose PSA velocity was greater than 0.35 ng/mL.

Percent free PSA or complexed PSA

PSA in the blood is either bound (attached) to proteins (known as complexed) or unbound (known as free). PSA assays usually measure the total PSA (both free and complexed). Other assays measure the percentage of free PSA or the percentage of complexed PSA. Compared with men who have BPE, men with prostate cancer have a higher percentage of complexed PSA and a lower percentage of free PSA.

Research suggests that determining the ratio of free to total PSA in the blood helps distinguish between PSA elevations due to cancer and those caused by BPE. Using the percent free PSA result to help determine the need for biopsy might help reduce the number of unnecessary biopsies.

Research suggests that in men with PSA levels between 4 ng/mL and 10 ng/mL, performing a prostate biopsy only when the percent free PSA is 24 percent or below would detect more than 90 percent of prostate cancers while reducing the number of unnecessary biopsies by 20 percent. Some investigators support using complexed PSA measurements to detect cancer, believing that this provides the same information as free PSA and total PSA.

Percent free or complexed PSA, as well as PSA density and PSA velocity, also can be used to determine the need for a repeat prostate biopsy when the initial biopsy shows no evidence of cancer but cancer is still suspected.

Age-specific PSA

PSA increases with age because the prostate gradually enlarges as men grow older. Some years ago, researchers suggested adjusting PSA levels to the age of the patient: Higher levels would be considered normal in older men, and lower levels considered normal in younger men. However, the concern is that the use of higher PSA thresholds in older men will miss important cancers. As noted previously, physicians should suspect prostate cancer at lower levels (above 2 ng/mL) or when PSA is rising at all in men in their 40s.

Understanding the TNM Cancer Staging System

The TNM (tumor, nodes, metastasis) staging system is used to describe a cancer's clinical stage, or how far it has spread. The system assigns a T number (T1 to T4) to describe the extent of the tumor as felt during a digital rectal exam (DRE). The N number (N0 to N1) indicates whether the cancer has spread to any lymph nodes, and the M number (M0 to M1) indicates the presence or absence of metastasis (spread to distant sites). The T and M designations are divided into subcategories (designated a, b and c) that provide further detail on the extent of the cancer. The TNM staging system is used to help determine appropriate prostate cancer treatment options (see "NCCN Risk Classification and Management Options" on page 43). ■

TNM	Description
T1	Tumor cannot be felt during DRE or seen with diagnostic imaging • T1a: Tumor found incidentally during surgery for benign prostatic hyperplasia (BPH) and is present in less than 5% of removed tissue • T1b: Tumor found incidentally during BPH surgery but involves more than 5% of removed tissue • T1c: Tumor found during needle biopsy for elevated PSA
T2	Tumor can be felt during DRE but is believed to be confined to the gland • T2a: Tumor involves one-half or less of one side of the prostate • T2b: Tumor involves more than one-half of one side but not both sides • T2c: Tumor involves both sides of the prostate
T3	Tumor extends through the prostate capsule and may involve the seminal vesicles • T3a: Tumor extends through the capsule but does not involve the seminal vesicles • T3b: Tumor has spread to the seminal vesicles
T4	Tumor has invaded adjacent structures (other than the seminal vesicles), such as the bladder neck, rectum or pelvic wall
N0	Cancer has not spread to any lymph nodes
N1	Cancer has spread to one or more regional lymph nodes (nodes in the pelvic region)
M0	No distant metastasis
M1	Distant metastasis • M1a: Cancer has spread to distant lymph nodes • M1b: Cancer has spread to the bones • M1c: Cancer has spread to other organs, with or without bone involvement

Source: National Cancer Institute.

Other biomarkers

Biomarkers are substances like PSA that can be measured in a body fluid and used to detect or monitor a disease. Prostate cancer researchers are testing several potential biomarkers to supplement the use of PSA in prostate cancer screening. One of these, proPSA (a precursor of PSA), has been shown to be useful in distinguishing between blood samples that have prostate cancer and those that do not. A urinary marker called PCA3 has also been useful in this regard. FDA approval for these tests is anticipated in the coming years.

It is likely that new markers, including the presence or absence of genetic variants, will be used in combination to predict the overall risk of prostate cancer, allowing better identification of those who should undergo a prostate biopsy.

Transrectal Ultrasound and Prostate Biopsy

If the results of a digital rectal exam, PSA test or both suggest cancer, transrectal ultrasound is performed to determine the size of the prostate, identify any areas that are suspicious for cancer, and to direct the needles used for prostate biopsy. A prostate biopsy typically takes about 15 to 20 minutes and is performed on an outpatient basis.

Doctors routinely use a local anesthetic such as lidocaine (Xylocaine) to reduce discomfort during the procedure. The ultrasound examination is performed with the man lying on his side.

An ultrasound probe (about the size of a finger) is gently inserted three to four inches into the rectum. The probe emits sound waves that are converted into video images corresponding to the different prostate zones. Small prostate cancers are usually not detectable by ultrasound examination.

Fitted to the ultrasound probe is a biopsy gun with a needle that is fired through the wall of the rectum. The needle extracts small pieces of prostate tissue in less than a second. Ideally, at least 10 to 12 tissue samples ("cores") are taken from the prostate. A pathologist examines the samples under a microscope to determine whether cancer is present.

If the prostate biopsy shows no cancer but the physician still suspects that cancer is present because of an abnormality on the digital rectal exam or PSA test, a repeat biopsy may be performed.

Each year, approximately one million prostate biopsies are performed in the U.S., and of those, about one in three are cancerous. About 5 to 10 percent of men who've had a biopsy will be told they have high-grade prostatic intraepithelial neoplasia (PIN). Formerly called dysplasia or atypical hyperplasia, PIN is believed to be a premalignant lesion. But recent studies suggest that the likelihood of finding cancer on a repeat biopsy is no greater in men with PIN

than in men with normal biopsy findings. Therefore, a finding of PIN alone is not a reason to perform a repeat biopsy.

About 5 percent of prostate biopsies reveal abnormal or atypical cells that suggest the possibility of cancer but are not sufficient to make a diagnosis. In such cases, a repeat biopsy is usually recommended because there is a 50 percent chance of finding cancer on that second biopsy.

If the biopsy results indicate cancer, additional diagnostic tests may need to be conducted to determine the extent of the disease (see below).

A prostate biopsy usually causes only minor discomfort. Common side effects include minor rectal bleeding; blood in the stool, urine or semen; and soreness in the biopsied area. All of these side effects disappear with time.

Additional Diagnostic Tests

Other routine diagnostic tests that will be performed include urinalysis and blood tests for anemia. If surgery is contemplated, general health status—particularly cardiovascular and pulmonary function—is assessed to determine whether the man is a suitable candidate for the procedure.

Determining the Extent of Cancer

Determining the extent of prostate cancer is important for predicting the course of the disease and in choosing the best treatment. Results from the digital rectal exam, PSA tests and prostate biopsy give the urologist a good idea of whether the cancer is confined to the prostate or has spread outside the gland.

The pathologist's examination of the biopsy specimen is crucial. After studying the characteristics of the tumor, the pathologist assigns a Gleason score to the cancer. The Gleason score provides an estimate of how aggressive the cancer is. Depending on the Gleason score and the initial PSA results, the physician may order imaging studies to determine whether the cancer has spread to distant sites.

The Gleason Score

The most important factor in predicting the current state of the prostate cancer and the success of any treatment is the Gleason score. This score is based on tumor grade, which is an indication of the tumor's aggressiveness. The tumor grade reflects how far the cancer cells deviate from normal, healthy cells. Normal prostate epithelial cells form highly organized glands, with well-defined borders. Cancer cells, in contrast, display various degrees of disorganization and distortion. Cancers whose cells appear closest to normal are considered grade 3 and generally are the least aggressive; those with highly irregular, disorganized features are classified as grade 4 or 5 and generally are the most aggressive.

The Gleason score is derived by determining the two most prevalent organizational patterns in the tumor, assigning each a grade, and then adding the two numbers together. For example, if the most common pattern—the primary grade—is 3 and the next most common pattern—the secondary grade—is 4, the Gleason score would be 7 or 3+4. But if the primary grade is 4 and the secondary grade is 3, the Gleason score would be 4+3, and this would be considered to be more aggressive. In other words, the primary grade carries more weight than the secondary pattern in determining the aggressiveness of the cancer.

In some cases the pathologist will report a tertiary pattern that is associated with prognosis but is not a part of the overall score. For example, a pathologist may report that the biopsy shows a Gleason 3+3 (score 6), with a tertiary pattern 4.

Most doctors classify a Gleason score of 6 as a low-grade tumor, a Gleason score of 7 as intermediate, and Gleason scores of 8, 9 and 10 as high grade. Gleason scores of 8 to 10 are associated with the least favorable outlook.

Imaging Studies

Some men will need to undergo a bone scan to determine whether their prostate cancer has spread to the bones. The bone scan involves intravenous injection of a radioactive substance that is preferentially taken up by the damaged bone. (Bone can be damaged by cancer as well as by osteoporosis and other bone diseases.) A special scanner is then used to detect the radioactivity. Areas of the body that show increased radioactivity have bone damage, possibly because cancer has spread to the bone.

A bone scan is not typically ordered when PSA levels are less than 10 ng/mL because the likelihood of cancer spread is very low. Men who have a PSA level of 20 ng/mL or higher, a Gleason score of 8 to 10, or disease extensive enough to be felt on both sides of the prostate or beyond the prostate should have a bone scan and a computed tomography (CT) scan of the pelvis.

The ProstaScint scan may be used to look for prostate cancer

cells that have spread to the lymph nodes or soft organs. It uses antibodies that attach to a protein called prostate-specific membrane antigen on prostate cancer cells. These antibodies mark cancer cells with a radioactive isotope that is then picked up by a special scanner. This scan is not considered very accurate, but it may be used when PSA levels start to rise again after surgery or radiation therapy.

If the digital rectal exam, PSA and Gleason score suggest that the cancer has spread, CT or magnetic resonance imaging (MRI) may be performed to look for enlarged lymph nodes. The urologist may recommend a laparoscopic biopsy. In this procedure, a surgeon uses a laparoscope (an instrument with a tiny light and camera) to view the lymph nodes near the prostate and take samples to check for cancer.

New approaches for detecting the presence or progression of prostate cancer are being investigated. These include positron emission tomography (PET) and PET/CT. Further development of these imaging procedures may provide more precise ways to diagnose recurrences and locate metastases (cancers that have spread).

After gathering this information, the physician can then describe the clinical stage (or extent) of the cancer. Clinical stage takes into account whether the cancer has spread to the lymph nodes, bones or other areas. One of two methods is used—the Whitmore-Jewett method or, more commonly, the TNM (tumor, node, metastasis) system (see "Understanding the TNM Cancer Staging System" on page 37).

Risk Classification

The National Comprehensive Cancer Network (NCCN), an association of 21 cancer treatment centers, convenes expert panels to make recommendations for diagnosis and treatment of cancers, including prostate cancer. The NCCN recommends that after a diagnosis of prostate cancer is made, the man should be categorized in one of four categories to help determine optimal management. The recognized categories are: very low risk, low risk, intermediate risk and high risk. The determination is based on PSA level, prostate size, needle biopsy findings and the stage of cancer (see "NCCN Risk Classification and Management Options" on page 43).

Choosing a Prostate Cancer Treatment

The choice of treatment for prostate cancer—active surveillance, surgery, radiation therapy or hormone therapy—depends on a man's prostate cancer risk category, his age and general health, and his personal preferences. For a disease in which there is no "best" choice, the man should play a large role in the decision-making process.

In healthy men with a life expectancy of more than 10 to 15 years, about 80 percent of prostate cancers detected by PSA testing are believed to have the potential to progress and thus warrant some type of treatment. Nevertheless, with increased use of PSA screening, some men will be diagnosed with small prostate cancers (which cannot be felt during a digital rectal exam but are confirmed by biopsy) of very low to low risk that pose no immediate threat and may never need treatment. Two recent studies suggest that 30 to 50 percent of cancers—depending on patient age—detected by PSA screening would never have become apparent if a prostate biopsy had not been performed.

Potential complications of the various prostate cancer treatments must be taken into consideration when deciding on a treatment plan. For example, if a man opts for surgery or radiation therapy, he risks the possibility of bowel, urinary or sexual problems. This is perhaps of even greater importance for older men with "favorable risk" (very low to low risk categories) prostate cancer, in whom the likelihood of complications from treatment outweigh the risk of dying of prostate cancer. This concern, coupled with the finding that many prostate cancers never need treatment, prompted the National Comprehensive Cancer Network (NCCN) to issue prostate cancer treatment guidelines recommending active surveillance (no treatment initially but continued careful monitoring) for men with very-low-risk prostate cancer who have a life expectancy of less than 20 years and for men at low risk when life expectancy is less than 10 years.

Doctors use several methods to help predict the seriousness of the cancer, which is factored into the treatment decision. For example, a Gleason score of 6 indicates a greater probability that the cancer is insignificant—and unlikely to grow rapidly and spread. Higher Gleason scores suggest a greater likelihood of a significant, life-threatening cancer.

Men with high-grade disease (Gleason score of 8 to 10) are considered poor candidates for active surveillance because of the presumed aggressiveness of their cancer. In addition to the Gleason score, the PSA level and the stage of the disease are used to stratify men into risk categories that help physicians determine the optimal management strategy (see "NCCN Risk Classification and Management Options" on page 43).

A man's age is also an important consideration when choosing

NCCN Risk Classification and Management Options

The choice of prostate cancer treatment is based in part on the likelihood, or risk, that your tumor will grow and spread to other parts of your body.

The lower your risk, the lower your chances that the prostate cancer will spread and that you will die of it. ■

Risk group	Newly diagnosed cases (%)	NCCN management recommendation
Very low • Stage T1c • Prostate-specific antigen (PSA) less than 10 ng/mL • Gleason score 6 or less and not more than two cores with cancer • Less than 50 percent of core involved with cancer • PSA density less than 0.15	15	• Active surveillance when life expectancy is less than 20 years.
Low • Stage T1c or T2a, and • PSA less than 10 ng/mL and • Gleason score less than 6	35	• Active surveillance when life expectancy is less than 10 years. • Active surveillance, surgery or radiation when life expectancy is more than 10 years.
Intermediate • Stage T2b-T2c or • PSA 10 to 20 ng/mL or • Gleason score 7	40	• Active surveillance or external radiation with/without hormonal therapy, with/without brachytherapy or surgery if life expectancy is less than 10 years. • Surgery or external radiation with/without hormonal therapy, with/without brachytherapy if life expectancy is 10 or more years.
High • Stage T3a or • PSA 20 ng/mL or higher or • Gleason score 8 or higher	10	• Surgery or radiation plus hormonal therapy.

Adapted from Mohler J, et al. NCCN Clinical Practice Guidelines in Oncology: Prostate Cancer. *Journal of the National Comprehensive Cancer Network.* 2010;8:162-200.

between active surveillance and a more aggressive treatment option. Because prostate cancer generally progresses slowly, active surveillance is less risky in older men with favorable risk disease. In fact, data show that men in their 70s and 80s who are diagnosed with very-low- to intermediate-risk prostate cancer are more likely to die of a cause other than their prostate cancer over a 10-year period—even without treatment. Men in their 50s and early 60s, in contrast, are more likely to live long enough for their prostate cancer to become life threatening. Prostate cancer experts at Johns Hopkins believe that the best candidates for active surveillance are over age 65 and have very-low-risk prostate cancers (see "NCCN Risk Classification and Management Options" on page 43).

Treatment Options for Prostate Cancer

Management options for prostate cancer are active surveillance, radical prostatectomy, radiation therapy, cryotherapy, hormone treatment and chemotherapy. One new option recently approved by the FDA is a type of immunotherapy.

Radical prostatectomy and radiation therapy can potentially cure prostate cancer when the disease is detected in its early stages. Radiation therapy can be delivered from an external source (external beam radiation therapy or EBRT) or by implantation of radioactive seeds (brachytherapy). Another option is cryotherapy (freezing the prostate). Although long-term data are lacking, early studies suggest that cryotherapy may be comparable to other therapies when used to treat men at low risk for disease progression. However, cryotherapy is not considered standard care by the NCCN. High-intensity focused ultrasound (HIFU) is an investigational treatment that has not been approved by the FDA but it is being used in Europe.

Hormone therapy is not curative and is generally used to slow the progression of the disease once it has spread to other sites. When prostate cancer is progressing despite hormonal therapy, the disease is referred to as castration-resistant prostate cancer (CRPC). Use of docetaxel (Taxotere) was found to offer a small survival benefit in men with CRPC.

Men who do not respond to Taxotere now have three additional options. One option is to use another chemotherapy agent, cabazitaxel (Jevtana), in combination with prednisone. Other options for men with CRPC include sipuleucel-T (Provenge)—the first immunotherapy agent approved by the FDA for cancer treatment—and abiraterone (Zytiga), a recently approved drug that blocks androgen within tumors. Both drugs offer a small survival benefit.

Because prostate cancer progresses more slowly than other types of cancer, men can take some time to carefully consider the treatment options, especially if they have a very-low- to low-risk cancer. A man should talk with his doctor about the relative risks and benefits of each option.

It is often useful to consult physicians from different fields (urologists, radiation oncologists and medical oncologists). This will help provide a broader spectrum of potential treatment opinions. Men with favorable risk prostate cancer typically have the most difficulty in making a management decision because they have more options from which to choose.

Active Surveillance

With active surveillance, a man opts to have no immediate treatment but undergoes close monitoring for cancer progression. This management approach is most often recommended for men with very-low- to low-risk prostate cancers that are believed to be small volume, especially older men whose cancers are unlikely to become life threatening during the remaining years of their life.

Experts at Johns Hopkins emphasize the importance of having adequate biopsy sampling before choosing active surveillance. If a man diagnosed with a cancer that appears suitable for surveillance had an initial biopsy that removed fewer than 12 cores of tissue, a repeat 12- to 14-core biopsy should be performed to confirm that more extensive or higher grade disease is not present before beginning active surveillance.

Men who choose active surveillance must see their doctor regularly and undergo testing to determine whether the cancer has progressed. How often a man who chooses active surveillance must see his doctor, and the tests he needs vary, depending on the physician and medical center. A typical follow-up plan requires a man to have a DRE and PSA test every three to six months, as well as a prostate biopsy no more than once a year. The triggers for intervention that most commonly prompt moving to treatment are a rising PSA or more cancer or a higher grade cancer on a surveillance biopsy.

Between visits, men who choose active surveillance should call their doctor if they experience any of the following symptoms: blood in the urine, difficulty urinating or new onset of pain. If tests reveal a man's prostate cancer has progressed, curative treatment options, such as radical prostatectomy or radiation therapy, may be considered at this point.

Radical Prostatectomy

Unlike surgery for BPE, which removes only the inner prostate tissue that is pressing on the urethra, radical prostatectomy removes

JOHNS HOPKINS
MEDICINE

LATEST RESEARCH

Which treatment for early prostate cancer?

Men under 65 with early-stage prostate cancer who undergo radical prostatectomy (RP) may be less likely to experience a recurrence or die of prostate cancer than their counterparts who adopt a "watchful waiting" approach, according to a study begun in 1989.

Between 1989 and 1999, the investigators randomly assigned 695 men with low-risk early-stage prostate cancer to watchful waiting or RP and followed them regularly for over a decade.

At a median of 12.8 years, 14.6 percent of men in the RP group died, compared with 20.7 percent in the watchful waiting group. The benefit was seen primarily in men younger than 65 and in men with low-risk tumors. For men over 65, 33 would need to undergo surgery to prevent one prostate cancer death.

Most of the men in this study had palpable tumors at diagnosis, which means that the cancers were more advanced than those identified today by PSA screening. Consequently, these findings may not be relevant for men with prostate cancer identified by PSA elevations. Results from two large studies that are under way should help clarify this. Active surveillance remains a viable choice for appropriately selected older men who have nonaggressive cancers that may never cause harm without treatment.

NEW ENGLAND JOURNAL OF MEDICINE
Volume 364
May 2011

State-of-the-Art Surveillance Strategies for Men on Active Surveillance

New methods help identify cancers that will need treatment

Doctors know that most prostate cancers diagnosed today are low grade and will grow slowly, if at all, over the course of 10 to 15 years. For many men facing such a diagnosis, aggressive treatment with prostate surgery or radiation therapy needlessly exposes them to risks, such as urinary incontinence and erectile dysfunction—problems that can seriously alter their quality of life.

These factors—coupled with research showing that delaying treatment in appropriately selected men does not compromise cure—underlie recent guidelines from the National Comprehensive Cancer Network (NCCN). The guidelines recommend active surveillance as a first-line option for older men at very low to low risk of developing advanced prostate cancer (see "Are You a Candidate for Active Surveillance?" on page 47).

Active surveillance requires a commitment to regular and intense prostate monitoring to allow doctors to determine if the cancer has become more aggressive—a sign that curative treatment should begin. Currently, doctors monitor tumor activity with regular digital rectal examinations (DRE), prostate-specific antigen (PSA) tests and surveillance biopsies. But researchers

are pushing the boundaries—searching for ways to identify seemingly low-risk cancers that have the *potential* to become more deadly. Findings from the Johns Hopkins active surveillance program—the largest and longest-running in the world—provide important insights.

Reclassifying risk

In one promising development, researchers were able to identify risk factors present at diagnosis and the first surveillance biopsy that were associated with disease progression and to use that information to restratify men into new risk categories. This strategy will make it possible for doctors to predict earlier and more accurately the likelihood that the cancer will progress after a man enters the surveillance program. And that information can help the patient decide whether active surveillance is something he still wants to pursue.

The findings, from a study of 376 men in the Hopkins surveillance group, were reported recently in *The Journal of Urology*. Here's a brief summary of the highlights:

• If a man's free PSA was greater than 15 percent and cancer was found on biopsy in less than 35 percent of any biopsy

core at diagnosis, his risk of reclassification to a higher risk category at the first follow-up biopsy 12 months later is 8 percent.

• If a man's free PSA was less than 15 percent and cancer was found in 35 percent or more of any biopsy core at diagnosis, his risk of reclassification at the first follow-up biopsy is 29 percent.

• If a man's PSA density, or PSAD (PSA divided by prostate volume), was below 0.08 and no cancer was found on the first surveillance biopsy, his risk of reclassification four years after entering the program was 11 percent.

• If the PSAD was 0.08 or higher and there was cancer on the first surveillance biopsy, his risk of reclassification jumped to 54 percent.

PHI + DNA = better predictions

Even when a cancer appears to be low risk, there is always a chance that it will grow and become more aggressive. One challenge is to determine the mathematical likelihood of that happening and to identify the men that it will happen to as early as possible.

To that end, researchers at Hopkins have been using a mathematical formula that helps predict which men in the active

the entire gland, along with the seminal vesicles and some of the surrounding tissue. It is the only treatment for localized prostate cancer (cancer confined to the prostate) that has been proven to reduce deaths from the disease when compared with no treatment.

Radical prostatectomy offers the possibility of a cure only if the

surveillance program will need treatment. Called the Prostate Health Index, or PHI, this mathematical equation takes into account PSA, percent-free PSA, and proPSA (a variant of PSA that increases in men with prostate cancer).

Using this information alone, they were able to predict with about 62 percent accuracy which men would have an unfavorable biopsy, meaning the finding of a higher Gleason score or greater volume of cancer on a surveillance biopsy. In addition, they performed a special DNA analysis of a patient's biopsied tissue. The combination of PHI and DNA analysis boosted the accuracy of the prediction to 70 percent.

For the study, the investigators followed 71 men in the active surveillance program who had banked blood and prostate tissue that had been obtained at diagnosis; 39 of them eventually had unfavorable biopsies.

After analyzing the men's baseline blood and biopsy samples, the researchers found that the PHI was higher in men who went on to develop unfavorable biopsies. In addition, the amount of DNA near where the cancer was found was also significantly higher in the men with unfavorable biopsy.

Are You a Candidate for Active Surveillance?

Based on data from the ongoing active surveillance program at Johns Hopkins that was initiated 16 years ago by Drs. Patrick Walsh, H. Ballentine Carter and Jonathan Epstein, active surveillance is most appropriate for men age 65 years and older with an expected lifespan of 15 to 20 years. Younger men with underlying medical ailments that will limit their life expectancy are also reasonable candidates.

To join the Hopkins active surveillance program, a man should have very low- to low-risk prostate cancer. Very-low-risk cancer meets all of the following criteria: stage T1c, a PSA less than 10 ng/mL, a Gleason score of 6 or less, no more than two cores with cancer, and with cancer involving less than 50 percent of any core and a PSA density less than 0.15. Low-risk cancer meets the following criteria: stage T1c or T2a, a PSA less than 10 ng/mL and a Gleason score less than 6.

In addition, the man must agree to have a digital rectal exam (DRE) and PSA test every six months and a 14-core prostate biopsy once a year, with two biopsy samples taken from the area of the prostate located farthest from the rectum (anteriorly).

Other active surveillance programs may have slightly different criteria for admission and follow-up.

Even though all men in the surveillance program appeared to be more alike than not—with similar Gleason grades, PSA levels and tumors—the combination of the PHI and DNA measurements categorized the study subjects with more specificity, improving the accuracy of predicting unfavorable biopsy conversion and providing a better means of identifying patients who may need treatment later.

Coming soon?

If you're on active surveillance or are thinking about it, keep in mind that these findings—though promising—need to be confirmed in larger groups before they move from the research setting to your doctor's office. For now, the safest, smartest strategy is for your doctor to monitor your cancer closely. And the only way to do that is for you to strictly adhere to the recommendations for follow up. ∎

---

cancer has not spread to the seminal vesicles, lymph nodes or to a distant site such as bone. As a result, when the risk of spread to lymph nodes is high, some surgeons perform a laparoscopic lymph node biopsy before the planned prostatectomy. However, because PSA testing is now widespread, it is uncommon to find cancer that has spread to the lymph nodes at the time of diagnosis.

Radical prostatectomy was not a favorable management option before the 1980s because of the high rate of ED and urinary incontinence associated with the procedure. But in the early 1980s, Johns Hopkins urologist Patrick Walsh, M.D., developed a new approach to the operation. He devised a "road map" that allowed surgeons to remove the prostate with less risk of damaging the nerves and tissues that are essential for erections and urinary control. (See "Nerve-sparing radical retropubic prostatectomy" on page 50). This anatomic approach has reduced the risk of severe incontinence to 1 to 3 percent and the risk of mild incontinence to around 10 percent.

The risk of ED varies according to a man's age, the quality of erections before surgery and the surgeon's skill at performing the procedure. The majority of men who have good-quality erections before surgery and a skillfully performed operation have return of erectile function sufficient for intercourse. Recovery can take more than a year in some instances. If recovery does not occur, ED can be treated successfully in most cases.

Rare complications of radical prostatectomy at the time of surgery include damage to the rectum or ureter (the tube carrying urine to the bladder from the kidneys) and the surgical and anesthetic risks that accompany any operation. Postoperatively, narrowing of the urethra (urethral stricture) by scar formation can cause a decrease in the force of the urinary stream or cause urinary retention. This is most likely to occur between one and three months after surgery.

After radical prostatectomy, PSA testing is performed to evaluate the success of the surgery and to monitor for disease recurrence. An undetectable PSA level (usually less than 0.2 ng/mL) after radical prostatectomy indicates that all the prostate tissue (both benign and malignant) has been removed. A detectable PSA immediately after surgery means that the tumor had already spread to other tissues before the surgery and thus could not be totally removed. A subsequent rise in PSA levels indicates that residual cancer that could not be removed at the time of surgery has grown to an extent that PSA production can be detected in the blood.

It usually is not possible to know whether the cancer is in the area of the prostate or at another site because the microscopic residual disease causing the elevated PSA cannot be seen with conventional radiographic imaging techniques.

For men with cancer confined to the prostate (stage T1 or T2) before treatment, the chance of a detectable PSA level indicating residual cancer 15 years after treatment is around 30 percent. A detectable PSA (biochemical recurrence) indicates the presence of residual prostate cancer months to years before the cancer would be visible on a CT or bone scan. For men with a biochemical recurrence, a recent study from Johns Hopkins demonstrates that the risk of dying of prostate cancer can be reduced by radiation therapy administered at the time of detectable PSA (salvage radiation therapy).

Hormone therapy would be considered for men with a biochemical recurrence, especially if the PSA doubling time is less than one year (indicating a rapidly growing cancer). On the other hand, a rising PSA more than two years after surgery in a man who showed no invasion of the seminal vesicles or lymph nodes at the time of surgery suggests that residual cancer is localized to the pelvis and that radiation therapy will more likely eradicate the disease.

Researchers at Johns Hopkins have studied the outcomes of men who had a detectable PSA after surgery. They monitored the course of nearly 2,000 patients whose cancer was confined to the prostate and who underwent radical prostatectomy performed by the same surgeon. Among the 304 men who had detectable PSA levels in the years following surgery, the five-year disease-free survival rate following the first detectable PSA level was 63 percent. Metastatic cancer (cancer that has spread to other parts of the body) was not apparent in these men for an average of eight years, and in those with metastatic disease, death from cancer occurred on average 13 years after PSA became detectable.

These results should reassure men who experience rising PSA levels following surgery. At the same time they serve as a reminder that continued monitoring is essential after surgery.

Recently, four centers joined forces to evaluate the risk of prostate cancer death among 23,510 men treated with radical prostatectomy from 1987 to 2005. The findings, which were published in *The Journal of Urology*, show that while the overall death rate at 15 years following radical prostatectomy was 7 percent, the cancer grade, presence of seminal invasion and the year of surgery were closely associated with the probability that a man would die of prostate cancer.

The investigators found that in general, the risk of death from prostate cancer increased directly with the Gleason score and with the extent of disease spread (see "Prostate Cancer Mortality after Radical Prostatectomy" on page 51). Men who underwent surgery in more recent years had a better prognosis than those who were operated on in earlier years. This is probably because smaller volume cancers were detected in more recent years and prostate cancer treatments have improved.

LATEST RESEARCH

Vigorous physical activity may boost prostate cancer survival

Vigorous physical activity may lower the risk of death from prostate cancer, new research suggests.

Investigators examined data from 2,705 men with prostate cancer who took part in the Health Professionals Follow-Up Study and were followed for 18 years. During the study, the men reported how much physical activity they performed each week, including cycling, running, walking and other exercises.

Any type of regular exercise improved overall survival, regardless of intensity. However, men who walked at least 90 minutes per week at a normal or brisk pace were 46 percent less likely to die of any cause than were men who walked less than 90 minutes per week at a slow pace.

What's more, men who reported taking part in vigorous activity—at least three hours of intensive exercise each week—had a significantly lower risk of dying of prostate cancer. Compared with men who exercised an hour a week or less, vigorous exercisers were 61 percent less likely to die of prostate cancer.

Exercise has well-known heart benefits, and these findings add to the mounting body of evidence that it's good for the prostate, too. If you haven't been exercising, start slowly and build up to a more vigorous level of activity.

JOURNAL OF CLINICAL ONCOLOGY
Volume 71, page 3889
June 1, 2011

Nerve-sparing radical retropubic prostatectomy

This procedure begins with a midline vertical incision in the abdomen—between the pubic area and the navel. (Some surgeons make the incision in the perineum, which is located between the scrotum and rectum; this rarely used approach is called a perineal prostatectomy.) If appropriate, samples of tissue from the pelvic lymph nodes may be removed and tested for signs of cancer. To minimize bleeding, which can obscure the surgeon's view and increase the risk of complications, the surgeon then cuts and ties off the group of veins that lie atop the prostate and urethra. Next, the surgeon severs the urethra, taking care to avoid the urethral sphincter muscles in order to preserve urinary continence.

At this point, the "nerve-sparing" aspect of the procedure comes into play. The prostate is dissected off of the rectum while tiny nerve bundles, known as neurovascular bundles, on either side of the prostate, are preserved, when possible. These neurovascular bundles are required to produce an erection.

The surgeon then cuts through the bladder neck (the junction between the bladder and the prostate) to completely separate the prostate and seminal vesicles from surrounding structures. Finally, the bladder neck is narrowed with stitches and reconnected to the urethra. A Foley catheter is inserted through the urethra to drain urine from the bladder. The catheter is left in place for about one to two weeks to allow the rebuilt urinary tract to heal.

Laparoscopic radical prostatectomy

Some surgeons use laparoscopy rather than open surgery to perform radical prostatectomy. Laparoscopy involves performing a procedure through small incisions in the abdomen using small instruments and a tiny camera. At present there appear to be few, if any, advantages of laparoscopy over open surgery.

A variation on the laparoscopic procedure is robotic-assisted laparoscopic radical prostatectomy, using the da Vinci robotic system. In this approach the surgeon performs the surgery by manipulating robotic arms that are attached to the laparoscopic instruments. When robotic-assisted surgery is compared with open surgery performed by a skilled surgeon, there are no differences in consumption of pain medications, time in hospital or time back to work. There also appear to be no differences in rates of return of urinary and sexual function.

When compared with men undergoing open surgery, men undergoing robot-assisted procedures may be more likely to regret

Prostate Cancer Mortality After Radical Prostatectomy[*]

Factor[+]	10-yr. mortality (%)	15-yr. mortality (%)	20-yr. mortality (%)
Age Less than 60 years			
Gleason score:			
6 or less	0.1	0.6	1.2
3+4	2.2	4.7	16
4+3	5.6	9	9
8-10	15	31	31
Organ confined	0.5	0.8	0.8
EPE	1.7	2.9	7
SVI	8.4	27	33
+LN	18	30	41
Age 60-69 years			
Gleason score:			
6 or less	0.1	0.2	0.2
3+4	1.7	4.2	9
4+3	4.4	11	23
8-10	13	26	39
Organ confined	0.5	1	1.4
EPE	1.9	3.9	6.6
SVI	8.8	22	26
+LN	12	22	42
Age 70-79 years			
Gleason score:			
6 or less	0	1.2	1.2
3+4	1.3	6.5	17
4+3	6.6	6.6	18
8-10	18	37	37
Organ confined	1.4	1.5	1.5
EPE	0.5	10	20
SVI	13	15	15
+LN	23	23	23

*Adapted from Eggener et al. *J Urol* 2011; 185:869-875. +Since these are estimates based on a number of factors that vary among individuals, a man's experience could be different from the rates in the table. Organ confined is a cancer completely confined to the prostate; EPE is extraprostatic disease or spread to the tissues around the prostate; SVI is seminal vesicle invasion; +LN is lymph node metastases.

their choice. Results from one study showed that men who underwent a robot-assisted procedure were three times more likely to be dissatisfied. This finding may be due to the unrealistic expectations that patients have when a manufacturer markets a "new" technology as being "minimally" invasive and without side effects.

Men who undergo laparoscopic removal of the prostate also may have lower rates of cancer control when compared with open surgery. A study in the *Journal of Clinical Oncology* found that when compared with open surgery, men who underwent laparoscopic surgery had a threefold greater risk of later needing an additional prostate cancer treatment. It's possible that recurrence rates might be higher for laparoscopic surgery because surgeons are unable to touch and feel the tissue, which may help determine when removal of additional tissue is necessary.

External Beam Radiation Therapy

This treatment involves aiming beams of radiation at the prostate from outside the body. It is a treatment option for men with localized prostate cancer (stage T1 and T2) or locally advanced disease (stage T3). Available evidence suggests that for patients with cancer confined to the prostate, either radical prostatectomy or radiation offers a good chance of being cancer free five to 10 years after treatment. Studies have shown that conventional-dose external beam radiation therapy coupled with hormonal therapy may prolong survival in men at increased risk for prostate cancer recurrence when compared with radiation alone. As with surgery, radiation therapy techniques have improved since the 1980s. Today, using three-dimensional imaging, radiation oncologists can now target the prostate more accurately and deliver higher dosages with fewer side effects.

External beam radiation therapy is also used as a palliative treatment. For a man with prostate cancer that has spread to the bones, radiation therapy can reduce pain and lessen the likelihood of bone fractures. It can also reduce neurological symptoms resulting from spinal cord compression when cancer has spread to the spine.

Radiation oncologists have made a number of refinements in external beam radiation therapy in an attempt to increase cure rates and reduce the risk of complications. These refinements include three-dimensional conformal radiation therapy (3DCRT), intensity-modulated radiation therapy (IMRT) and proton-beam radiation.

In 3DCRT, the radiation oncologist relies on dozens of images to target the radiation precisely to the tumor. This allows higher doses of radiation to be delivered (potentially increasing the treatment's effectiveness) and causes less damage to healthy tissue (potentially reducing the severity of treatment side effects).

IMRT is a refinement of 3DCRT. Relying on computer software to determine the orientation, number and intensity of the radiation beams, IMRT can improve the precision of 3DCRT.

Proton-beam radiation therapy is delivered in the same manner as 3DCRT but uses positively charged subatomic particles (protons) instead of photons to kill cancer cells. One recent study in the *Journal of the American Medical Association* (*JAMA*) found that men with early prostate cancer who received high-dose combined proton and traditional radiation therapy were more likely than men receiving standard-dose treatment to have PSA levels suggesting they were cancer-free after 10 years. However, both groups had the same risk for side effects. Experts seem to agree that proton beam radiotherapy is ideal for some types of tumors but is not more effective than IMRT for prostate cancers.

The complications of radiation therapy are primarily adverse effects on the urinary tract and bowel. However, these effects usually disappear days to weeks after treatment is completed. The risk of long-term urinary complications, such as blood in the urine, bladder irritation or narrowing of the urethra, is about 8 percent. The risk of long-term rectal complications, such as rectal inflammation (proctitis), bleeding, ulceration, narrowing and chronic diarrhea, is about 3 percent. A recent study found that men who were treated with radiation therapy for prostate cancer have a higher risk than the general population of developing rectal cancer, suggesting that they should be monitored for the disease.

With radiation therapy the risk of ED becomes more likely with time. In an analysis from the Prostate Cancer Outcomes study, 63 percent of men treated with radiotherapy had ED five years after the treatment. Younger men and those with normal sexual function before radiation therapy are the most likely to maintain potency, just as with surgery.

A postradiation PSA level greater than 0.5 to 1 ng/mL strongly suggests that some cancer remains; rising PSA levels after radiation therapy are evidence of disease progression. If cancer recurs after radiation therapy but there is no evidence of metastasis, some patients benefit from removal of the prostate or from cryotherapy. Hormone therapy is used to treat recurrent disease at distant sites.

Brachytherapy

In brachytherapy, another type of radiation treatment for prostate cancer, 80 to 120 radioactive seeds (tiny metal pellets) are implanted directly into the prostate through the skin between the scrotum and rectum under ultrasound guidance. The pellets emit radiation for several months. After their radioactive energy is spent, they remain

JOHNS HOPKINS
MEDICINE

LATEST RESEARCH

Radiation therapy for localized prostate cancer

High-dose intensity-modulated radiation therapy (IMRT) is well tolerated and is associated with excellent long-term tumor-control outcomes in men with localized prostate cancer.

IMRT allows doctors to safely deliver high doses of radiation to the prostate and seminal vesicles while delivering lower doses to adjacent healthy tissue. Researchers administered high-dose radiation (81 Gy) to 170 men with low-, intermediate- or high-risk disease.

At 10 years, 81 percent of the low-risk group, 78 percent of the intermediate-risk group and 62 percent of the high-risk group had not experienced a biochemical recurrence. In addition 100 percent of the low-risk group, 94 percent of the intermediate-risk group and 90 percent of the high-risk group were free of distant metastases.

Post-radiation erectile dysfunction was reported in 44 percent of the men who were potent before treatment. In addition, there was a 16 percent risk of developing late genitourinary side effects and a 5 percent risk of developing delayed gastrointestinal side effects that required medication or a minor procedure.

If you have localized prostate cancer and are considering IMRT, these findings provide evidence of its long-term effectiveness and help clarify the long-term risks.

CANCER
Volume 117, page 1429
April 2011

harmlessly in the body. Since the pellets are not removed and emit radioactivity over months, this approach is called permanent low-dose-rate brachytherapy.

Brachytherapy is appropriate for men with early-stage, localized prostate cancer (very low to low risk). The procedure may not be as effective as radical prostatectomy or external beam radiation therapy for men with higher-grade tumors or more advanced stages of disease. Consequently, an expert panel recently recommended against using brachytherapy in men with stage T2 or higher cancers, Gleason scores of 7 or more or PSA levels above 10 ng/mL. Some physicians recommend a combination of EBRT and brachytherapy for men with more advanced disease, but the combination may increase the risk of bowel-related side effects.

The side effects of brachytherapy are similar to those of EBRT—urinary and bowel problems—but these complications may occur more often with brachytherapy among men with very large or very small prostates, those with lower urinary tract symptoms that are bothersome and those that have previously had a transurethral prostatectomy (TURP). In addition, the radioactive seeds can migrate to other parts of the body, such as the lungs, although research suggests that seed migration has no negative consequences.

Another technique, high-dose-rate brachytherapy, is a refinement of low-dose-rate brachytherapy. In high-dose-rate brachytherapy, radioactive pellets are delivered to the prostate via hollow plastic needles. The pellets emit a high dose of radiation over a 24- to 48-hour period, after which they are removed.

Available research suggests that outcomes are similar among men treated with high- or low-dose-rate brachytherapy. But men treated with the newer technique experienced fewer side effects, including less urinary frequency, incontinence, blood in the urine and rectal pain.

When radiation therapy is used to treat intermediate or high-risk prostate cancer, hormonal therapy should be used in combination because survival is longer when compared to the use of radiotherapy alone. The timing of the hormonal therapy is usually short term (four to six months) during and after treatment of intermediate disease, and longer (two to three years) during and after treatment of high-risk disease.

Hormone therapy is sometimes given to men with larger prostates (greater than 40 g, or about 1.5 oz.) who are scheduled to start brachytherapy, with the aim of shrinking the prostate before the radioactive pellets are implanted.

Cryotherapy

Also known as cryoablation or cryosurgery, cryotherapy is a treatment that kills cancer cells by freezing them. In the procedure, thin needles (cryoprobes) are inserted through the perineum (the area between the scrotum and anus) and into the prostate. Needle placement is guided with an ultrasound probe placed in the rectum. Freezing gases drop the temperature of the cryoprobes to about -40° C. The extremely low temperatures create ice balls that freeze the entire prostate and some of the nearby tissue. Warm saline is circulated through the urethra and bladder to protect them from the freezing temperatures.

Cryotherapy may be a reasonable option for men whose cancer is contained within the prostate, and it is sometimes used when radiation therapy has failed to destroy the cancer. The risk of ED is high with cryoablation and its long-term effectiveness is less certain than that of surgery or radiation therapy.

Hormonal Treatment

Male sex hormones (androgens), especially testosterone, are required to maintain the size and function of the prostate. As a result, a treatment option for intermediate and high risk prostate cancers is to interfere with the effects of androgens by blocking the testicles' production of testosterone or blocking the receptor to which testosterone attaches. Hormonal therapy causes the cancer to regress, and is used routinely with radiation therapy for treating intermediate- and high-risk cancers and in the management of metastatic prostate cancer. When used for the treatment of metastatic prostate cancer, prostate cancer cells eventually bypass the testosterone block by manufacturing their own needed androgens through alternate pathways. Therefore, although hormone therapy is useful in treating prostate cancer, it does not offer a cure.

Hormone therapy used to be reserved for men whose prostate cancer had spread to the lymph nodes, bone or other sites. Now it is often given preemptively to men whose cancer is expected to spread; for example, a man with a rapidly rising PSA level.

For men with metastatic prostate cancer (spread to lymph nodes or bone), the goals of hormone therapy are to prolong life and relieve symptoms such as bone pain or urinary tract problems. In general, men whose cancer has metastasized have the following survival times: 75 percent live less than five years, 15 percent live five to 10 years, and 10 percent live more than 10 years.

PSA level helps predict survival in men with metastatic prostate

Medications Used in the Hormone Treatment of Prostate Cancer 2012

Drug type: Brand (generic)	Average daily dosage*	How to take
Estrogens		
Premarin (estrogen, conjugated)	1.25-2.5 mg 3x per day	At the same time every day.
Luteinizing hormone-releasing hormone (LHRH) agonists		
Eligard, Lupron (leuprolide)	*Lupron:* 7.5/22.5/30 mg injected every 1, 3 or 4 months, respectively *Eligard:* Same as above and 45 mg injected every 6 months	*Lupron:* Injected intramuscularly by doctor. *Eligard:* Injected subcutaneously by doctor into varying sites.
Trelstar Depot (triptorelin) Trelstar LA (triptorelin) Trelstar (triptorelin)	3.75 mg injected every month 11.25 mg injected every 3 months 22.5 mg injected every 6 months	Injected intramuscularly by doctor.
Zoladex (goserelin)	3.6 mg injected every month or 10.8 mg injected every 3 months	Injected by doctor into abdomen.
Luteinizing hormone-releasing hormone (LHRH) antagonists		
Firmagon (degarelix)	240 mg, then 80 mg injected every month	Injected subcutaneously into abdomen by doctor.
Antiandrogens		
Casodex (bicalutamide)	50 mg daily	At the same time every day, with or without food. Used with an LHRH analog.
(flutamide) (generic only)	750 mg daily	Two 125-mg tablets every 8 hours. Used with an LHRH analog.
Nilandron (nilutamide)	300 mg daily for 30 days, then 150 mg daily	With or without food. Used in combination with LHRH analogs or surgical castration, because antiandrogens are not as effective when used alone.
CYP17 inhibitor		
Zytiga (abiraterone)	1,000 mg per day	On an empty stomach. Do not eat two hours before or one hour after taking Zytiga. Used in combination with prednisone, 5 mg taken orally twice daily.

* These dosages represent an average range for the treatment of prostate cancer. The precise effective dosage varies from person to person and depends on many factors. Do not make any changes to your medication without consulting your doctor.

LHRH = luteinizing hormone-releasing hormone; LH = luteinizing hormone

How they work	Precautions	Most common side effects	Call your doctor if...
Blocks the release of (LHRH) from the hypothalamus, preventing the action of (LH), which signals the testicles to produce testosterone.	If estrogen is discontinued, testosterone levels will return to normal. Do not take if you have liver disease. May increase risk of cardiovascular problems, including heart attack and blood clots.	Breast enlargement, nausea, vomiting, fluid retention, erectile dysfunction, loss of libido.	You develop sudden changes in vision or speech, severe headaches, leg pains, dizziness or faintness.
Initially, these drugs stimulate the pituitary to release LH, prompting a jump in testosterone production. After several weeks, they block LH formation, and testosterone levels fall to castrate range.	May cause a temporary increase in cancer symptoms such as pain, urinary blockage or weakness of the legs. May increase risk of diabetes, cardiovascular disease. (Pose less cardiovascular risk than estrogens.) Your doctor should monitor you for these conditions.	Sweating, hot flashes, weight gain, fatigue, erectile dysfunction, loss of libido, loss of bone and muscle mass, headache, transient increase in cancer symptoms (see at left), mild pain, bruising or itching at injection or implant site.	*Eligard, Lupron:* You develop hives; rash; itching; difficulty breathing or swallowing; numbness, tingling, weakness or pain in the feet or lower legs; painful or difficult urination; blood in urine; bone pain; testicular or prostate pain; inability to move arms or legs. *Trelstar and Zoladex:* You develop rash, itching, swelling, severe dizziness, trouble breathing, sudden severe headache, vomiting or visual changes soon after injection.
Blocks the production of gonadotropin-releasing hormone (GnRH) by the pituitary gland, which prevents GnRH from stimulating the testes to produce testosterone.	Tell your doctor if you have any heart, kidney or liver problems or problems with the balance of your body salts or electrolytes. Can elevate liver enzymes; liver function should be tested during use.	Pain, redness and swelling around the infection site; hot flashes; flushing of the skin; weight gain; fatigue; increase in some liver enzymes.	You gain weight unexpectedly, feel more tired than usual, experience back or joint pain, develop chills or symptoms of a urinary tract infection, have decreased sex drive or erectile dysfunction.
Antiandrogens bind to the same cellular receptors that androgen hormones (including testosterone) use to stimulate prostate cells. Thus, they prevent androgen hormones from affecting the prostate.	Known to cause liver damage; liver function must be checked. May interact with several drugs, including cholesterol-lowering medications and anticoagulants such as warfarin. *Nilandron:* Risk of lung damage; a routine chest X-ray is required before first dose. May cause trouble adjusting to the dark.	Hot flashes, pain in the back or pelvis, diarrhea. *Nilandron:* constipation.	You experience nausea, vomiting, abdominal pain, fatigue, loss of appetite, flu-like symptoms, dark urine, jaundice, tenderness in your right upper abdomen. *Nilandron:* Seek immediate attention if you develop shortness of breath, coughing, chest pain or fever.
Inhibits an enzyme the body needs to produce testosterone from cholesterol.	Tell your doctor if you have a history of heart or liver disease, or problems affecting the adrenal or pituitary glands. Increases in liver enzymes may occur, requiring a change of dose or discontinuing use.	Joint and muscle pain, swelling, hot flashes, diarrhea, urinary tract infections, frequent urination, elevated blood pressure, abnormal heart rhythm, heartburn, cough and cold-like symptoms.	You experience dizziness, rapid heartbeats, faintness or lightheadedness, headaches, confusion, muscle weakness, pain or swelling in your legs or feet.

cancer. A PSA of less than 4 ng/mL within three to six months of initiating hormone therapy predicts a good response to the treatment. A rising PSA level during hormone therapy indicates that the disease is progressing.

No consensus exists concerning when hormone therapy should begin. Whether hormone treatment is started before or after cancer progression is documented on a bone scan may or may not affect how long a man survives. Moreover, all effective forms of hormone therapy have significant side effects. These side effects may include ED (which affects about 90 percent of men), loss of libido, breast enlargement, weight gain, hot flashes, loss of muscle mass, osteoporosis (decreased bone mass), fatigue and a decline in cognitive function. Hormonal therapy also increases the risk of cardiovascular disease in some men, and the harm may outweigh the benefit, especially for men with localized cancer who are unlikely to experience improved cancer control when hormonal therapy is used in addition to other management options. Because no hormone treatment can cure the disease regardless of when treatment begins, treatment side effects must be given serious consideration when deciding when to start the treatment.

There are many options for hormonal therapy of prostate cancer. Surgical castration (surgical removal of the testicles, which produce about 95 percent of a man's testosterone) was the main approach prior to the 1980s. Today the most common approach is the use of medications that either interfere with the production of testosterone by the testicles (medical castration) or block it from attaching to receptors inside cancer cells. These medications include estrogens; antiandrogens; luteinizing hormone-releasing hormone (LHRH) agonists, also known as gonadotropin-releasing hormone (GnRH) agonists; and LHRH antagonists, also known as GnRH receptor antagonists (see "Medications Used in the Hormone Treatment of Prostate Cancer 2012" on pages 56-57).

When prostate cancers progress despite hormonal therapy, the cancer is referred to as "castrate resistant," at which point chemotherapy is given to prolong life. Whether accomplished surgically or medically, hormone therapy prolongs the life of men with metastatic prostate cancer.

In April 2011 the FDA approved the drug abiraterone (Zytiga) for the treatment of castrate-resistant prostate cancer that no longer responds to chemotherapy. The approval was based on results from a trial that showed an average increase in survival of four to five months among men who took abiraterone compared to placebo. The

new drug works by blocking the synthesis of testosterone precursors in the testicles and adrenal glands, and also within the cancer cells (see "Abiraterone for Metastatic Castrate-Resistant Prostate Cancer" on pages 64-65).

Surgical castration

Surgical removal of the testicles, a procedure known as bilateral orchiectomy, was the first method used to treat metastatic prostate cancer. The operation can be performed in about 20 minutes under spinal or local anesthesia.

The effect of orchiectomy is almost immediate. Within 12 hours, testosterone levels plummet to what is known as the castrate range. This approach is not often used today because there are equally effective methods for reducing testosterone without the need for surgery.

Medical castration

It is also possible to interfere with the body's production of testosterone using medications that disrupt the process. The signal to produce testosterone originates in an area of the brain called the hypothalamus. At regular intervals the hypothalamus secretes luteinizing hormone-releasing hormone (LHRH), which stimulates the pituitary gland to produce luteinizing hormone (LH) and follicle-stimulating hormone (FSH). LH signals specialized cells in the testicles (Leydig cells) to secrete testosterone into the bloodstream; FSH stimulates sperm production in the testicle. Some testosterone is produced by the adrenal glands (paired organs that lie above the kidneys) but not enough to support maintenance of the prostate. When testosterone reaches the prostate it is converted to dihydro-testosterone (DHT)—a more potent form of testosterone—by the enzyme 5-alpha-reductase. The drugs used for medical castration inhibit this sequence of events at various stages.

Estrogen preparations. A synthetic form of the female hormone estrogen can lower testosterone levels to the castrate range by blocking the release of luteinizing hormone from the pituitary gland. Daily doses of synthetic estrogen (Premarin) are as effective as surgical castration, although the hormone takes longer to work, with testosterone levels falling over a two-week period.

Estrogens are rarely used today because of side effects that increase the risk of heart attack, stroke, blood clots in the legs or lungs, inflammation of the veins (phlebitis) and swelling (edema) of the legs.

Locally Advanced Prostate Cancer: Who to Treat with Radiation and Hormones?

New research provides important answers—for now

In the past two decades, doctors have come a long way in their understanding of how to best treat locally advanced prostate cancer. One effective treatment has been external beam radiation, or EBRT. Studies have shown that men who undergo EBRT have a good chance of being cancer-free five to 10 years after treatment.

Investigators have tried to improve upon that record by incorporating hormone therapy into the treatment plan. And this one-two punch—with hormone therapy given first to shrink and sensitize the tumor, followed by EBRT to destroy the cancer cells—has improved survival—so much so that today, hormonal therapy before, during and after EBRT in some cases has become the standard of care, but only for men with more aggressive locally advanced disease.

What doctors had been less certain about is whether men with less aggressive cancers will also benefit from combination therapy. New research has begun to provide needed clarification.

RTOG 94-08

The first published findings establishing a benefit of combination therapy for men with intermediate-risk disease were reported in the *Journal of the American Medical Association* in 2008. Results from a study published last year in the *New England Journal of Medicine* provide additional support for those results.

Known as RTOG (Radiation Therapy Oncology Group) 94-08, the study began in 2004 and involved nearly 2,000 men with early localized prostate cancer and a prostate-specific antigen (PSA) level of 20 ng/mL or lower. These were the characteristics associated with the most favorable prostate cancer prognosis at the time the study was initiated.

The men were randomly assigned to treatment with either radiotherapy alone or radiotherapy plus short-term androgen deprivation therapy (ADT). Men who underwent short-term ADT received flutamide orally (250 mg) three times a day plus a monthly injection of goserelin (Zoladex, 3.6 mg) or leuprolide (Lupron and others, 7.5 mg) for four months. Radiotherapy began after the second month of the four-month-long ADT regimen.

The investigators found that the overall 10-year rate of survival was 62 percent for the radiotherapy-plus-ADT group compared with 57 percent for those who received radiotherapy alone. The combination treatment also significantly lowered the rate of death due to prostate cancer and reduced the rates of biochemical failure, distant metastases and positive findings on repeat biopsy. Further analysis of the study data

LHRH agonists. Also known as gonadotropin-releasing hormone (GnRH) agonists, LHRH agonists are synthetic agents with chemical structures almost identical to natural LHRH. Initially, they behave like LHRH and stimulate the release of luteinizing hormone from the pituitary gland, which causes an increase in testosterone production. But after a short period they block the release of luteinizing hormone and reduce testosterone secretion from the testicles. The result is testosterone levels similar to those that occur after surgical castration or with estrogen. LHRH agonists are equivalent to surgical castration and estrogen in their ability to delay progression of cancer and prolong survival.

Commonly used LHRH agonists are goserelin (Zoladex), leuprolide (Eligard, Lupron), and triptorelin (Trelstar). LHRH agonists are traditionally given as injections monthly or up to several

revealed that these improvements were seen primarily in men with intermediate-risk prostate cancer. Their overall survival was 72 percent compared with 66 percent for those who only had radiotherapy.

Among men with low-risk disease, the addition of short-term ADT did not significantly increase the 10-year rate of overall survival or death from prostate cancer. As a result, the investigators concluded that ADT plus EBRT was not justifiable in men with low-risk prostate cancer.

Part of the rationale for not using combination treatment in these men has to do with the possible cardiovascular risks associated with Zoladex, Lupron and other luteinizing hormone-releasing (LHRH) agonists. In late 2010, the U.S. Food and Drug Administration (FDA) required LHRH drugs to carry new labels warning that these medications could pose a

small but increased risk of heart attack, stroke, sudden death and diabetes. These risks are particularly relevant to men with known heart failure or a previous heart attack or both.

Even in men with intermediate- or high-risk prostate cancer, the cardiovascular risks of hormone therapy must be weighed against the benefits. And a man with a history of heart disease or who is obese, issues that can increase his risk of heart troubles, must address them before he starts hormone therapy—if the treatment is to be used at all. That means taking heart-healthy steps, such as stopping smoking, losing weight if overweight or obese, and keeping blood pressure and cholesterol under control.

New techniques call for new answers

Although these findings provide more clarification about exactly

which men with localized prostate cancer are likely to benefit from combination therapy with hormones and radiation, they may not be the final word.

That's because the radiation doses and techniques used in RTOG 94-08 are no longer used today. Currently, because of more precise radiation techniques, such as three-dimensional conformal radiation therapy and intensity-modulated radiation therapy (see page 52), men with intermediate risk prostate cancer can now be given higher doses of radiation with less concern about damaging healthy tissue near the prostate.

Ultimately, the use of newer radiation techniques could mean that there is no need for hormone therapy to shrink the tumor. Another study, RTOG 08-15, is under way to evaluate newer high-dose radiation methods in men with intermediate-risk prostate cancer. ∎

months, depending on the dosage. Another option is an implanted drug delivery system (Viadur) that releases leuprolide continuously for one year.

The initial increase in testosterone with LHRH agonists may be severe enough to increase bone pain in men with prostate cancer that has spread to the bones. This can be prevented with an anti-androgen (see page 62) until testosterone levels fall to the castrate range about two to three weeks later.

Other side effects of the LHRH agonists include ED, loss of libido, hot flashes, weight gain, fatigue, and decreased bone and muscle mass. (The bisphosphonates pamidronate [Aredia] and zoledronic acid [Zometa] have been shown to prevent bone loss associated with LHRH agonists, and zoledronic acid may actually boost bone density.) Some men experience irritation at the injection sites. LHRH agonists are less likely than estrogen to cause breast enlargement, nausea, vomiting or cardiovascular problems.

LHRH antagonists. LHRH antagonists, also known as GnRH receptor antagonists, work by targeting and blocking luteinizing hormone receptors in the pituitary. This causes the testicles to decrease testosterone production.

The newest LHRH antagonist is degarelix (Firmagon), which was approved by the FDA in 2008 for use in men with advanced prostate cancer. The medication has been shown to begin working more quickly than the LHRH agonist leuprolide and to be equally effective at reducing testosterone levels. Another advantage of Firmagon over LHRH agonists is that it doesn't appear to cause a temporary surge in testosterone levels at the start of treatment.

The most common side effects are pain and swelling at the injection site, hot flashes, weight gain and signs of liver abnormalities on lab tests. These abnormalities generally improve when the medication is stopped.

Antiandrogens. To stimulate prostate cells (both cancerous and noncancerous), testosterone must first bind to specific androgen receptors ("docking sites") on the cells. Drugs called antiandrogens can occupy these receptors, preventing testosterone from binding to them and stimulating the cells. Because antiandrogens do not block testosterone production—a characteristic that sets them apart from the other types of hormone therapy—erectile function may be preserved in some patients. Three antiandrogens are approved by the FDA to treat advanced prostate cancer: bicalutamide (Casodex), flutamide (available only as a generic) and nilutamide (Nilandron).

When used alone, antiandrogens may not be as effective as medical or surgical castration. In addition, antiandrogens can cause hot flashes, breast enlargement, diarrhea and, in rare instances, liver damage. Men taking an antiandrogen must have their liver function tested a few months after starting treatment. Signs of liver problems include nausea, vomiting, fatigue, and jaundice. Nilandron may slow the eyes' ability to adapt to darkness. This side effect lasts about four to six weeks.

In 40 to 75 percent of men taking an antiandrogen, PSA levels increase, indicating disease progression. If the medication is discontinued, PSA levels fall. Why this occurs is not clear. Some researchers theorize that a mutation in the cancer cells causes them to respond to antiandrogen stimulation.

Total androgen blockade. The adrenal glands also produce small amounts of androgens, including testosterone. In an attempt to

eliminate all androgen stimulation of cancer cells, some doctors use antiandrogens along with surgical or medical castration. The combination of an antiandrogen (to block the effect of adrenal androgens) and castration (which halts testosterone production in the testicles) is referred to as total androgen blockade or total androgen suppression.

Despite promising preliminary findings, numerous studies have failed to demonstrate that total androgen blockade prolongs life any better than blocking testicular androgens alone. For example, a recent analysis of numerous studies found no difference in survival between men treated with total androgen blockade and those who underwent surgical castration or took LHRH agonists alone. Similarly, the largest clinical trial to date of total androgen blockade found no survival advantage among men treated with total androgen blockade (orchiectomy plus flutamide) compared with those treated with orchiectomy alone.

The inability of total androgen blockade to arrest cancer progression is probably due to the ability of cancer cells to manufacture needed androgens using precursor forms of androgens and other mechanisms that may bypass the need for androgens altogether. Progress in the discovery of these mechanisms that allow a prostate cancer to become castrate resistant have improved and will continue to improve the survival of men with advanced disease.

Intermittent androgen suppression. In this approach, androgen is blocked chemically (using an LHRH agonist or gonadotropin-releasing hormone antagonist alone or in combination with an antiandrogen) until PSA levels fall. Treatment is then discontinued until PSA levels begin to climb again. The rationale for this approach is the belief that hormone therapy encourages the growth of cancer cells that become castrate resistant.

Some doctors believe that cycling therapy on and off (intermittent androgen suppression) may delay the emergence of these deadly cells. This practice is associated with fewer side effects because the therapy is discontinued for periods of time. More studies are needed to determine whether intermittent androgen suppression is as effective at slowing disease progression as continuous androgen suppression. Nonetheless, many oncologists routinely use this approach.

Other options. Testosterone levels can be reduced within 24 hours with the drug ketoconazole (Nizoral). The drug is approved by the FDA to treat fungal infections but it also inhibits the production of adrenal and testicular androgens. Nizoral is used only when lowering androgens rapidly might be beneficial (to alleviate pain, for example).

Abiraterone for Metastatic Castrate-Resistant Prostate Cancer

New hope for men with advanced disease

At some point following surgery or radiation treatment for prostate cancer, 30 percent of men receive the upsetting news that their PSA is rising. This is a signal that some cancer cells have been left behind following surgery, were resistant to radiation or had previously escaped and are now multiplying. Many men with residual cancer will require additional treatment, but most will not need androgen deprivation therapy (ADT) to lower testosterone.

But if cancer spreads to distant sites, ADT can bring about significant long-term control of the cancer by blocking male hormones called androgens, particularly testosterone, which fuel tumor growth. Blocking these hormones causes PSA to drop significantly and the cancer to regress in most men.

Some men do extremely well with ADT, but for others, the cancer cells learn to grow in the presence of low testosterone levels. The cancer cells eventually begin to proliferate. PSA levels start to rise, or there is evidence of bone metastases detected by X-ray. No longer held in check by hormonal therapy, the cancer continues to spread.

This phase of the disease is known as metastatic castrate-resistant prostate cancer. For many years, there was little doctors could do for a man who had reached this point, but that is beginning to change.

Entering the era of hope
In the space of a year, the therapies available for men with metastatic castrate-resistant prostate cancer jumped from one to four. Docetaxel (Taxotere), was approved by the Food and Drug Administration (FDA) for prostate cancer treatment in 2004. It remained the only option until 2010 when sipuleucel-T (Provenge) and cabazitaxel (Jevtana) were approved, and they were followed in 2011 abiraterone (Zytiga).

The availability of so many options makes this an extraordinary time of hope for men with advanced disease. And that hope—for patients and researchers alike—is to turn advanced castrate-resistant prostate cancer into a chronic disease rather than a terminal one.

The most recent drug to be added to the armamentarium, Zytiga, works by inhibiting the activity of two key enzymes involved in testosterone synthesis, effectively blocking testosterone production throughout the body—not only in the testicles but also in the adrenal glands and the prostate cancer cells themselves. For years, researchers have considered androgens produced by the adrenals or prostate cancer cells to be unimportant, but that does not appear to be true.

In the pivotal 1,195-patient study of Zytiga, which was reported in the *New England Journal of Medicine,* investigators reported that 797 patients randomly chosen to take Zytiga (1,000 mg per day) plus prednisone (5 mg per day) lived an average of 15 months compared with 11 months for a control group treated with prednisone plus a placebo.

Nothing to crow about?
Some may question the value of Zytiga and the other new drugs, not only because they don't "cure" but also because study results for all the therapies showed what might be considered only modest improvement in survival. For example, Zytiga increased survival

In addition, it is used only in the short term because it raises luteinizing hormone levels, which can cause rising testosterone levels and lead to disease progression. Nizoral can also cause liver problems.

A new hormonal therapy, abiraterone (Zytiga), is available for men with advanced prostate cancer who no longer respond to medical castration and have already been treated with the chemotherapy drug Taxotere (see "Abiraterone for Metastatic Castrate-Resistant Prostate Cancer" above).

by only four months.

On the surface, the results look like "nothing to crow about." But the findings were actually so impressive that the study was stopped early, and the men who were taking placebo were allowed to switch to Zytiga. One reason for the kudos: Zytiga reduced testosterone in the blood to levels never seen before—less than 1 ng/mL, which is perhaps why the drug works.

This is certainly a groundbreaking medication for several reasons. First, it provided significant benefit for two-thirds of study subjects with advanced and aggressive prostate cancer that has left the prostate gland.

In addition, most men experienced significant benefits for an average of eight months, with PSA levels plummeting and tumor size decreasing. What's more, Zytiga completely alleviated pain in men who had significant pain complaints due to the spread of cancer to their lymph glands and bones.

Last, but definitely not least, Zytiga and the other drugs were studied in men whose tumors had progressed after treatment with other therapies, and who had just a few months to live.

Now that the drugs are FDA-approved, they will be given to patients with early-stage disease, with the hope and expectation that survival time will be much greater.

Different lines of attack

Part of the beauty of these new treatments is that each one acts in a totally different way, giving doctors multiple unique methods of attacking the cancer. Taxotere is a chemotherapy drug that kills a significant number of cancer cells—though not all of them. The population of cells that is not killed will take varying amounts of time before they finally return, depending on how stressed these cells become.

Jevtana is a second-line therapy employed to slow disease progression after other chemotherapy drugs, including Taxotere, have stopped working. Jevtana works by crippling cancer cells so that they can no longer divide properly.

Provenge is a novel option—a therapeutic vaccine given to men with advanced prostate cancer to get their own immune systems to attack and eliminate the cancer.

Once circulating in the body, Provenge alerts the body's immune system to seek out, attack and destroy prostate cancer cells wherever they are lurking.

Consider a clinical trial

Even though there are now several therapeutic options, with each new addition come questions about the best management strategies. For example, which of the drugs should be used at which point in the disease progression? And in what order? Currently, there are no good scientific data to guide treatment decisions.

You may want to consider participating in a clinical trial that could help provide answers and potentially lead to the development of newer, more effective therapies for metastatic castrate-resistant prostate cancer. Clinical trials are sponsored by government agencies, medical institutions, pharmaceutical companies, foundations and other organizations. Most are listed at Clinicaltrials.gov, a searchable database maintained by the National Institutes of Health. ■

Chemotherapy

Chemotherapy can help relieve pain and other symptoms associated with advanced prostate cancer that no longer responds to hormone therapy. Until recently, attempts to slow disease progression and improve survival with chemotherapy had proved disappointing. But several clinical trials have now provided evidence that docetaxel (Taxotere) plus estramustine (Emcyt) or prednisone can prolong survival in men whose advanced prostate cancer no longer responds to hormone therapy. Although the survival advantage gained by using chemotherapy is modest—a few months—these landmark studies are prompting renewed research into chemotherapy's potential to affect the disease, not just ease its symptoms. For example, the chemotherapy drug cabazitaxel (Jevtana) was approved in June 2010 for the treatment of advanced prostate cancer that continues to worsen despite treatment with Taxotere.

Symptom Relief

When hormone therapy loses its effectiveness (cancer is castrate resistant), other treatments are available to relieve cancer pain and improve quality of life. A wide range of medications—nonsteroidal anti-inflammatory drugs and corticosteroids, as well as morphine and other narcotics—may be used to ease pain. Mitoxantrone (Novantrone)—a chemotherapy drug used to treat a form of leukemia—is also approved for reducing pain from metastatic prostate cancer. Novantrone is used in combination with the corticosteroid prednisone. Using Taxotere and prednisone together can also reduce pain and improve quality of life.

Bone pain can be treated with medications known as bisphosphonates (such as zoledronic acid [Zometa]), radiation therapy, or injections of a radioactive substance called strontium-89. For a man whose prostate has not been removed, transurethral resection of the prostate (TURP) can relieve urinary tract symptoms from locally advanced disease.

Immunotherapy

A new option for treating prostate cancer that no longer responds to hormone treatment is immunotherapy. The agent sipuleucel-T (Provenge) is a vaccine made in a laboratory from a patient's own white blood cells. Provenge, which was approved by the FDA in May 2010, works by targeting prostatic acid phosphatase, an antigen expressed by most prostate cancers.

Although Provenge does not appear to stop the spread of prostate cancer, it improves survival in some men. The extra time is modest; in one 512-person trial, survival averaged about 26 months for men taking Provenge compared with 22 months for those taking a placebo.

However, Provenge offers proof that a cancer vaccine to boost the immune system can prolong life, suggesting that future vaccines might be even more effective. Furthermore, investigators at Johns Hopkins and other institutions are studying whether Provenge can

increase the effectiveness of other treatments, such as radiation and androgen deprivation therapy. Studies are also underway to determine if immunotherapy may be an effective intervention in men who have earlier-stage prostate cancer that has a high risk of relapse after standard treatments.

Managing Treatment Side Effects

The two side effects of prostate cancer treatment that concern men the most are urinary incontinence and ED. Osteoporosis (thinning of the bones) also is a problem because it can lead to decreased mobility, reduced quality of life and debilitating falls.

As treatments for prostate cancer improve, these complications will become less common. For now, however, men should be aware that there are effective ways to help alleviate the problems they may experience.

Urinary Incontinence

Surgery or radiation therapy may irritate the urethra or bladder or damage the urinary sphincter (muscles that contract to prevent urine from flowing out of the bladder). As a result, some degree of incontinence (inability to control bladder function) is common after treatment.

Urge incontinence (the strong and sudden need to urinate, followed by a bladder contraction and involuntary loss of urine) is common for a few days after catheter removal in men who have undergone TURP for the treatment of BPE. However, in the initial period after radical prostatectomy for prostate cancer, men typically experience stress incontinence, in which urine leakage occurs during moments of physical strain (such as sneezing, coughing or lifting heavy objects).

Recovering bladder control can be a slow process and may take up to six months. Fortunately, severe incontinence occurs in less than 1 percent of men after surgery for BPE and in fewer than 3 percent of men following radical prostatectomy or radiation therapy for prostate cancer.

Several approaches can be taken to improve bladder control. These include lifestyle measures, Kegel exercises, collagen injections, and surgical implantation of an artificial sphincter or placement of a urethral sling. In addition, the use of absorbent products, penile clamps, external collection devices, catheters and medications also can help men cope with incontinence resulting from treatment.

Lifestyle measures

Simple changes in diet and behavior can be helpful. Excess weight increases pressure on the bladder and worsens incontinence. Weight loss through calorie restriction and increased physical activity will help. Because constipation can worsen symptoms, it is important to eat high-fiber foods, such as leafy green vegetables, fruits, whole grains and legumes. Caffeine and alcohol increase urinary frequency and should be limited. If nighttime urination is a problem, avoid consuming liquids during the last few hours before bed.

Kegel exercises

These exercises are performed by squeezing and relaxing the pelvic floor muscles that surround the urethra and support the bladder. To locate the pelvic floor muscles, try slowing or stopping your urine flow midstream as you urinate. Strengthening these muscles may improve bladder control after radical prostatectomy.

In one study, 19 percent of men who performed regular Kegel exercises had regained urinary continence by one month, and 95 percent of the men were continent by six months. Among men who did not do the exercises, 8 percent were continent by one month, and 65 percent were continent by six months.

A recent study in the *Journal of the American Medical Association* also reports benefits from Kegel exercises (see "Behavioral Therapy for Post-prostatectomy Incontinence" on pages 70-71).

Collagen injections

If urinary incontinence persists, injection of a synthetic collagen-like material around the bladder neck to add bulk can provide increased resistance to urine leakage during times of physical strain. Repeat injections often are needed because these materials are gradually broken down by the body.

Surgical treatments

Placement of an artificial urinary sphincter (a doughnut-shaped rubber cuff) around the urethra is a treatment for more severe urinary incontinence after prostate cancer surgery. The cuff is filled with fluid and connected by a thin tube to a bulb implanted in the scrotum. The bulb in turn is connected to a reservoir implanted within the abdomen. The fluid in the cuff creates pressure around the urethra to hold urine inside the bladder.

When a man feels the urge to urinate, he squeezes the bulb. This transfers fluid from the cuff to the reservoir and deflates the cuff for three minutes so that urine can drain through the urethra. Afterward, the cuff automatically refills with fluid and urine flow is again impeded.

Urethral sling procedures are another form of surgical management of incontinence and are usually used for less severe cases. The sling is made of synthetic material and lifts and compresses the urethra, thereby preventing urinary leakage.

Absorbent products

Wearing absorbent pads or undergarments is the most common way to manage incontinence. These products are often used right after surgery and are effective for managing all degrees of incontinence, ranging from mild to severe. These products are ideal for men who have minimal leakage on occasion.

Penile clamps

An option for severe incontinence, penile clamps compress the penis and urethra to prevent urine from leaking. However, penile clamps are not recommended immediately after treatment because they interfere with the development of the muscle control needed to regain urinary continence.

External collection devices

These condom-like devices can be pulled over the penis and held in place with adhesive Velcro straps or elastic bands. A tube drains urine from the device into a bag secured on the leg. Collection devices should not be used immediately after surgery when men are attempting to regain urinary control.

Catheters

A Foley catheter is a small tube that is inserted through the urethra to allow urine to flow continuously from the bladder into a bag. This option is not recommended for long-term use because it can cause irritation, infection and, possibly, loss of bladder muscle control.

Medications

Although medication can be used to help control mild to moderate incontinence, it is not effective for severe cases. Drugs such as oxybutynin (Ditropan) and tolterodine (Detrol) may reduce urge incontinence by decreasing involuntary bladder contractions. Other options

ASK THE DOCTOR

Q. *My doctor told me the caffeine in my coffee is causing me to get up frequently during the night to go to the bathroom. Is that true?*

A. There's no doubt about it, caffeine stimulates increased urination. Coffee, tea and chocolate belong to a family of drugs called theoxanthines. Coffee (caffeine) and tea (theophylline and caffeine) can directly irritate the bladder and the prostate as well as increase the amount of urine output through their diuretic effect on the kidneys, increasing the volume of urine and the rate of urine production. If the bladder is already sensitive or overactive, rapid filling tends to lower the threshold for contractility, creating an urge to urinate more frequently, although in smaller volumes.

There are excellent decaffeinated products available to replace regular tea and coffee. You should consider these, as well as herbal teas or fruit and vegetable juices. If you are a heavy coffee or tea drinker, you may experience a period of withdrawal, similar to a prolonged hangover, which will last two or three days. But this usually passes on its own, and the need for coffee and tea will diminish.

Behavioral Therapy for Post-prostatectomy Incontinence

Is it worth a try?

Urinary incontinence is a relatively common complication following radical prostatectomy, depending on the definition used; but its impact on a man's quality of life can vary considerably. Most men eventually regain total control requiring no protection. Men who experience few episodes with smaller amounts of urine loss tend to describe their symptoms as bothersome. For men with more frequent episodes or greater urine loss, however, the effects can be profound. For some, incontinence—or even fear of an episode—can lead to avoidance or discontinuation of daytime activities, sleep deprivation and disruption of sexual activity. Over time, it can chip away a man's physical and mental well-being.

A recent study in the *Journal of the American Medical Association* detailed the success of an eight-week behavioral therapy program for men with long-standing post-prostatectomy urinary incontinence, and it may be worth a try. But you'll need to have realistic expectations about what it can accomplish.

Study specifics
For the study, 208 men, ages 51 to 84, whose incontinence persisted from one to 17 years after their radical prostatectomy, were randomly assigned to one of three groups:

• Group 1: Men in this group—behavioral therapy only—had one office visit with an incontinence specialist every other week for eight weeks. During sessions they received instruction on pelvic floor muscle strength training (Kegel exercises) and learned bladder control strategies; for example, how to use Kegels to avoid accidental incontinence episodes while standing, lifting and laughing. They also received advice on fluid management, such as avoiding all caffeine-containing drinks, since caffeine contributes to urinary frequency. The men were instructed to perform the exercises and use bladder control strategies each day and to keep a daily voiding and intake diary.

• Group 2: Men in this group received the same behavioral therapy instruction as those in group 1, but they also had in-office biofeedback sessions and used an electrical stimulation device at home. Biofeedback involved performing pelvic muscle exercises while connected to a machine that measures the strength and effectiveness of muscle contractions to help a man identify the pelvic floor muscles.

• Group 3: Men in this group kept bladder diaries for the first eight weeks. After that time, the men could choose to begin behavioral therapy with or without biofeedback.

A look at the results
At the end of the eight-week period, group 1 experienced a 55 percent reduction in incontinence episodes, from 28 down to 13 per week. In addition, 55 percent of the men reported wearing fewer pads or diapers than before treatment. What's more, 90 percent described their leakage as "better" or "much better" overall, and 16 percent achieved complete continence.

Group 2 experienced a 51 percent reduction in incontinence episodes, dropping from 26 to 12 per week. In addition, 42 percent of the men in group 2 reported wearing fewer pads or diapers than before treatment, 91 percent described their leakage as "better" or "much better" overall, and 17 percent achieved complete continence.

Group 3 had a 10 percent reduction in episodes, dropping from 25 to 20 each week. Only 5 percent of the men in group 3 reported wearing fewer pads or diapers, 10 percent described their leakage as "better" or "much better," and 6 percent achieved complete continence.

A closer look
Among men in groups 1 and 2, incontinence episodes dropped

include nasal decongestants such as pseudoephedrine, or the antidepressant imipramine (Tofranil), which can reduce stress incontinence by increasing smooth muscle tone in the bladder neck.

Because pseudoephedrine is a stimulant that can increase heart

from 28 to 13 per week and from 26 to 12 per week, respectively. While that improvement is impressive, when the findings are looked at another way, it means that these men were still experiencing about two episodes per day. Further, 38 percent of the men in groups 1 and 2 reported using the same number of urinary protection pads at the end of eight weeks as they had used at the beginning of the study. In addition, 84 percent of the men in group 1 and 83 percent of the men in group 2 failed to achieve complete continence

The bottom line

Clearly, behavioral therapy with or without biofeedback can improve post-prostatectomy incontinence in some men. The similarity of results between the men in group 1 and group 2, however, demonstrate that the addition of biofeedback and electrical stimulation to behavioral therapy does not significantly improve outcome.

In addition, it's important to understand that there is a very good chance behavioral therapy will not lead to complete continence. Most experts believe that pelvic floor muscle training may shorten the time to urinary control after surgery but that it does

---

Pelvic Floor Muscle Training: Kegel Exercise Tips

Repeated contractions of the pelvic floor muscles, also called Kegel exercises, are the cornerstone of the behavioral program because they may increase the function of muscles involved in urinary control.

Incontinence experts recommend performing Kegels before and after your radical prostatectomy. The good news: They're not difficult to learn how to do. Here are a few tips.

Start in the bathroom. As you begin urinating, try to stop or slow the urine stream without tensing the muscles of your legs, buttocks or abdomen. It is important not to use those other muscles because only the pelvic floor muscles help with bladder control.

When you are able to stop or slow the stream of urine, you have located the proper muscles. Feel the sensation of the muscles pulling inward and upward.

What about when you're not urinating? If you're having trouble locating the muscles that need strengthening, imagine that you're in a crowded elevator and need to pass gas. The muscles that you automatically tighten up to keep gas from escaping are the same muscles that are used in Kegel exercises.

Once you've identified the proper muscles, follow the instructions below:

• Perform sets of eight to 12 maximal contractions and hold each contraction for 5 to 10 seconds.

• At the end of each set, perform five to 10 rapid contractions.

• Perform the exercises five times each day.

Kegel exercises can also be helpful when you're in a situation where you might experience leakage. For example, if you feel a sneeze coming on, perform the Kegel maneuver to avoid urine leakage while you sneeze.

As with all your other muscles, you'll need to keep exercising your pelvic floor muscles regularly to maintain tone. That means continuing with at least one set of Kegels per day even after you've stabilized.

---

not affect the overall outcome since men destined to become dry would eventually have done so without exercising.

With that caveat, there's nothing harmful about behavioral therapy, so it's certainly worth a try—it could reduce your incontinence episodes and improve your quality of life. ◼

---

rate and blood pressure, it should only be used under a doctor's supervision. The drug may cause nervousness, restlessness and insomnia and may have adverse effects in people with asthma or cardiovascular disease.

Erectile Dysfunction

Men who undergo radical prostatectomy or radiation therapy for prostate cancer often fear they will be unable to resume sexual activity after treatment. Although these procedures may result in ED, they do not directly affect libido or the ability to achieve orgasm. This is in contrast to hormone therapy, which lowers testosterone levels and decreases libido. Several options are available to help men regain lost sexual function.

The penis is made up of nerves, smooth muscle and blood vessels. Within the penis are two cylindrical chambers—called the corpora cavernosa or corporal bodies—that extend from the base to the tip. When a man has an erection, smooth muscle tissue within the penis relaxes, causing these spongy chambers to dilate and fill with blood. The swollen corporal bodies press against and close the veins that normally allow blood to flow away from the penis; as a result, the penis remains engorged with blood. After orgasm, the smooth muscle tissue contracts and blood once again exits the penis.

This process is initiated by signals passing through nerve bundles that run along both sides of the prostate toward the penis. Radical prostatectomy can lead to ED if one or both of these nerve bundles is damaged during surgery. Nerve damage does not affect sensation in the penis, but it does impair a man's ability to achieve or maintain a normal erection. Radiation treatment also can result in ED by damaging these nerve bundles or the arteries that carry blood to the penis.

The first treatment used in ED is usually an oral medication. If medication is ineffective or inappropriate, other options include vasodilators (drugs that dilate blood vessels), which are injected or inserted into the penis, and vacuum pumps. Surgical implantation of a prosthesis is an option for men who do not regain sexual function with less invasive forms of treatment.

Oral medications

Three oral medications for ED are available: sildenafil (Viagra), vardenafil (Levitra) and tadalafil (Cialis). These medications are unlike other ED therapies because they do not produce erections in the absence of sexual stimulation. Normally, sexual arousal increases levels of a substance called cyclic guanosine monophosphate (cGMP) in the penis. Higher levels of cGMP relax smooth muscles in the penis and allow blood to flow into its two inner chambers.

Viagra, Levitra and Cialis work by blocking the actions of an enzyme called phosphodiesterase type 5 (PDE5), which is found primarily in the penis. PDE5 causes erections to subside by breaking down cGMP. By maintaining increased cGMP levels, the three drugs (known as PDE5 inhibitors) enhance both the relaxation of smooth muscles in the corpora cavernosa and the engorgement of these chambers with blood. As a result, men with ED can respond naturally to sexual arousal.

Oral drugs have been tested in a wide range of men with ED. It is not known whether one drug is better than another because the medications have not been compared directly.

Viagra and Levitra are effective for about four hours. Cialis, however, is effective for 24 to 36 hours, making it more convenient and allowing more spontaneity in a man's sexual relationship. Cialis is also now available for daily use in a 2.5-mg or 5-mg dose. Daily Cialis is an appropriate choice for men who anticipate having frequent sexual activity.

Men who take alpha-blockers need to check with their physician before using a PDE5 inhibitor. Levitra cannot be used with alpha-blockers. Viagra can be used, but not within four hours of taking an alpha-blocker. Cialis can only be used with Flomax—and only at the 0.4-mg per day dosage of Flomax.

PDE5 inhibitors have a number of other potential drug interactions and side effects and must be used with caution in men who have cardiovascular disease.

Vasodilators

Erections can be produced with vasodilators, medications that expand the blood vessels and allow the penis to become engorged with blood. The most commonly prescribed vasodilator for ED is alprostadil. Other vasodilators include papaverine and phentolamine.

Alprostadil can be injected directly into the base of the penis with a needle or inserted into the urethra in pellet form. Both approaches have drawbacks. Injections can cause discomfort, scarring and, rarely, priapism—a painful, prolonged erection that must be treated medically. The pellet form, known as the MUSE delivery system, can cause burning in the urethra. Using low doses of alprostadil can minimize the risk of these side effects.

Because vasodilators cause erections by dilating blood vessels—an event that occurs after the nerve signals travel from the nerve bundles to the penis—these medications may work when a PDE5 inhibitor does not. For instance, vasodilators may be effective for men whose nerve bundles are damaged or no longer intact. The injections also may be helpful when used in conjunction with an oral ED medication. Moreover, researchers theorize that regular

JOHNS HOPKINS
MEDICINE

ASK THE DOCTOR

Q. *I understand that erectile dysfunction (ED) can be a complication after surgery or radiation therapy for prostate cancer, but are there any differences?*

A. The difference between post-radiation therapy-induced ED and post-prostatectomy-induced ED is simply timing: Men who undergo radical prostatectomy find that their ability to achieve an erection suitable for penetration is lost immediately. Over time—and it can take up to two years—they can regain their full capacity for erections.

By comparison, for men who undergo radiation therapy, erections remain intact for the first year or two if androgen deprivation therapy (hormonal therapy) is not part of the radiation treatment. Over the next two to four years, however, their erections may slowly decline. That's because radiation affects the nerves that trigger erections as well as the arteries and veins that supply the penis, and this damage takes time to appear.

The good news is that oral ED medications are helpful, regardless of which treatment is performed.

injections of vasodilators (regardless of whether the injections are followed by sexual activity) might promote the return of normal erections, presumably by re-establishing blood flow to the penis. Based on this theory, many doctors are recommending a more aggressive approach to ED, with treatment beginning shortly after surgery.

Vacuum pumps

A simple, noninvasive treatment for ED is the vacuum pump—an airtight tube that is placed over the penis before intercourse. The tube is attached to a pump, which withdraws air from the tube and creates a partial vacuum that causes the penis to become engorged with blood. A constricting ring is then placed at the base of the penis to prevent blood from flowing back out.

Erections last approximately 30 minutes. Leaving the constricting ring on for a longer period may be harmful. Vacuum pumps are highly effective devices, but many men find them cumbersome and inconvenient.

Surgery

Several types of surgically implanted devices can provide erections sufficient for sexual intercourse. One, a semi-rigid device (a silicone rod inserted into the penis), is folded upward close to the body until a man is ready for sexual intercourse. Just before intercourse, he bends the device into the erect position.

A more commonly used device consists of two hollow cylinders implanted into the penis, a reservoir placed in the lower abdomen and a pump placed in the scrotum. To achieve an erection, the man squeezes the pump to move fluid into the cylinders in the penis.

Osteoporosis

Men treated with hormone therapy for advanced prostate cancer are at high risk for developing osteoporosis—fragile bones due to loss of bone mineral density. Men's bones may actually take a double hit because prostate cancer tends to spread to the bones and weaken them. When that happens, the cancer is typically treated with androgen-deprivation therapy, which further contributes to bone loss because androgens help maintain bone density in men.

Research suggests that men can lose two to six percent of their bone mineral density in the first year of androgen-deprivation therapy. Bone loss continues in the second year but at a much slower rate. Bone loss can result in painful fractures and falls, loss of mobility and independence and a reduced quality of life.

Men with other osteoporosis risk factors are at greater risk for complications. General risk factors for osteoporosis include white race, thin build, lack of weight-bearing exercise, cigarette smoking and alcohol consumption.

To detect osteoporosis early, men with advanced prostate cancer should undergo regular bone-density screening with dual-energy X-ray absorptiometry (DEXA) scanning.

If your doctor determines that you have osteoporosis, effective medications are available to strengthen and protect your bones. First-line therapy is usually a bisphosphonate, such as alendronate (Fosamax) or zoledronic acid (Reclast), which slows the breakdown of bone. Some men may benefit from a selective estrogen receptor modulator (SERM), including raloxifene (Evista) or toremifene (Fareston). These drugs stimulate bone building and shut down the activity of osteoclasts, which destroy bone. Finally, a promising new drug called denosumab (Prolia) blocks the formation of a protein that causes bone to break down. A study published in the *New England Journal of Medicine* found that Prolia reduced the risk of vertebral fractures by 62 percent.

PROSTATITIS

Prostatitis is a common condition in which the prostate becomes infected or inflamed. The disorder may cause severe pain in the perineum (the area between the rectum and scrotum). Men may also feel pain in their groin, genitals and lower back.

Another possible symptom is an urgent or frequent need to urinate, which is sometimes mistakenly attributed to benign prostatic enlargement (BPE), also referred to as benign prostatic hyperplasia (BPH). Some men complain of painful ejaculation but others report that ejaculation relieves pain. According to one study, some men with prostatitis have a quality of life so diminished that it is comparable to that of men who have recently suffered a heart attack.

Prostatitis is often difficult to treat, in part because several forms of the disease exist and the cause of the most common form is unknown. Some men experience acute flare-ups caused by a bacterial infection of the prostate. This acute bacterial prostatitis is associated with a sudden and continuous pain that lasts for several days. Some men have signs of inflammation, such as white blood cells in their semen, but not the painful symptoms of prostatitis.

More common, however, is chronic prostatitis, which can arise from a bacterial infection or an unidentified nonbacterial source. Nearly 95 percent of men with prostatitis are believed to have the chronic non-bacterial form (also known as chronic prostatitis/chronic pelvic pain syndrome, or CP/CPPS). Chronic nonbacterial prostatitis may last for several weeks or longer, only to disappear and then flare up again.

Causes of Prostatitis

The cause of bacterial prostatitis is obvious and easy to detect—infection with some type of bacteria. But researchers are not sure why some men develop the more common, nonbacterial form.

The current thinking is that an initial trigger, either within the prostate or the pelvis where the prostate is located, promotes inflammation. Then the nerves that are affected by this inflammation are sensitized and inappropriately send pain messages that persist long after the trigger has disappeared. Trigger events could be anything causing inflammation in or around the prostate, such as an infection within the prostate, trauma to the perineal area (for example, from riding a bicycle) or a prostate biopsy.

Some researchers suggest that chronic prostatitis is not a prostate problem at all. They attribute flare-ups to a pelvic muscle spasm or some other factor that mimics symptoms originating in the prostate.

Another theory is that prostatitis is an autoimmune disorder in which the immune system mistakenly attacks healthy prostate tissue and promotes inflammation.

Recent evidence suggests that any of these problems or a combination of them can trigger chronic prostatitis. Once the chronic pain syndrome is initiated, flare-ups could be triggered by many things such as stress, emotional problems, or certain foods or beverages, like coffee. Other possible culprits include urinary tract abnormalities, infrequent ejaculation, dysfunctional urination, lower urinary tract infection, trauma to the perineal area (for example, from riding a bicycle) and inflammation. None of these potential causes of nonbacterial prostatitis has been confirmed by solid research.

Diagnosis of Prostatitis

As part of the initial evaluation for prostatitis, a urine sample is evaluated to determine whether the disease stems from a bacterial infection. If chronic prostatitis is suspected, a urine sample may be taken from a man's normal urine flow and then from urine voided after a prostate massage (in which the doctor strokes the prostate until fluid is pushed into the urethra). However, the value of these pre- and postmassage urine cultures has been questioned. When the diagnosis is not clear-cut—which is often the case—other diagnostic tests will need to be performed.

Treatment of Prostatitis

Treatment for bacterial prostatitis is fairly straightforward: antibiotics for at least four weeks. Appropriate antibiotics include trimethoprim/sulfamethoxazole (Bactrim), doxycycline (Doryx) and fluoroquinolones such as ciprofloxacin (Cipro). Bacterial prostatitis is the most curable form of the disease. That said, some men do not respond to treatment and symptoms sometimes reappear once the antibiotics are stopped.

Treatment of nonbacterial prostatitis is more difficult. Some experts now believe that there are six CPPS subtypes, which are based on the presence of certain symptoms or characteristics. They propose that treatment or treatments (combination therapy is often required to obtain sufficient relief) be individualized based on the man's particular subtype(s). These include:

Urinary symptoms. Pain on urination as well as a bothersome increase in urinary frequency and urgency and/or nighttime urination. Possible treatments include anticholinergic medications such as tolterodine (Detrol) and oxybutynin (Ditropan); alpha-blockers such as tamsulosin (Flomax) and alfuzosin (Uroxatral); and dietary changes such as cutting down on caffeine, spicy foods and alcohol.

Psychosocial symptoms. A history of anxiety, depression, stress and/or a history of sexual abuse. Counseling, cognitive behavioral therapy, stress reduction techniques, and an antidepressant may be effective in this setting.

Organ-specific symptoms. Pain localized to the prostate or pain that is associated with filling and emptying the bladder. Therapies to address these symptoms include pentosan polysulfate (Elmiron), dimethyl sulfoxide (DMSO) and botulinum toxin (Botox) administered directly into the bladder. Alternative therapies such as quercetin, bee pollen, bromelain/papain and saw palmetto (Permixon), as well as neuromodulation also may be helpful.

Infection. Infection caused by organisms not typically associated with bacterial prostatitis. Ideally, the urine should be cultured to

LATEST RESEARCH

Promising therapy for chronic prostatitis

Men with chronic pelvic pain who fail to find relief with traditional treatments may benefit from an intensive six-day combination physical therapy-behavioral treatment that targets pelvic muscle tenderness.

Researchers evaluated the protocol, known as myofascial trigger point therapy and paradoxical relaxation training (PRT), in 116 men who had pelvic pain for a median of 4.8 years. Trigger point therapy, which involves applying pressure on a trigger point in a tight muscle until it "releases," was performed by a physical therapist for 30 to 60 minutes daily for five consecutive days. A psychologist provided daily instruction in PRT for three to five hours. The goal of PRT is to reduce nervous system arousal in the presence of perceived pain and catastrophic thinking. The men were instructed to use the techniques at home.

At six months, their quality of life had improved significantly, and 82 percent of the men reported improvement in pain and urinary dysfunction. The improvement was described as major or moderate by 59 percent and as slight by 23 percent.

If you have chronic pelvic pain with pelvic muscle tenderness that has not improved with standard medical therapies, consider asking your doctor for a referral to physical and behavioral therapists with experience treating this condition.

THE JOURNAL OF UROLOGY
Volume 185, page 1294
April 2011

identify a causative organism and the infection treated with an anti-biotic that the infectious organism is known to be sensitive to. If an antibiotic is prescribed before specific culture results are obtained and the patient does not respond to adequate therapy, an additional course of antimicrobial therapy is not warranted.

Neurological conditions. The presence of other pain-related neurologic or systemic conditions, such as irritable bowel syndrome or low back and leg pain. Neuroleptic drugs, such as pregabalin (Lyrica), nortriptyline (Aventyl, Pamelor) and amitriptyline, and acupuncture are potential therapies. Referral to a pain management clinic and stress reduction techniques also may be beneficial.

Skeletal muscle tenderness. The presence of spasms or trigger points in the abdomen or pelvis on examination by the doctor. Potential treatments for skeletal muscle tenderness include pelvic floor physical therapy, stress reduction, behavior modification (for example, sitting on a cushion when seated for a long period), oral antispasmodics, and neuromodulation. ■

GLOSSARY

5-alpha-reductase inhibitors— A class of drugs used to treat benign prostatic hyperplasia (BPH). They block the conversion of testosterone into dihydrotestosterone, the major male sex hormone within the cells of the prostate.

active surveillance—A method of managing prostate cancer in which a man is closely monitored, but curative treatment is not initiated until the cancer progresses.

acute urinary retention—A complete inability to urinate that requires immediate medical attention.

age-specific PSA—An adjustment of the PSA value that accounts for the natural, gradual increase in PSA that occurs with age as the prostate enlarges.

alpha-1-adrenergic blockers—A class of drugs used to treat benign prostatic hyperplasia (BPH) that work by relaxing smooth muscle in the prostate. Also called alpha-blockers.

androgens—Sex hormones, such as testosterone, found in higher levels in males than females.

antiandrogens—Drugs that bind to androgen receptors in cells, preventing androgens from stimulating the cells.

benign prostatic hyperplasia (BPH)—Noncancerous enlargement of the prostate gland due to an increase in the number of prostate cells.

bladder neck—The junction between the bladder and the prostate.

brachytherapy—A prostate cancer treatment that involves implanting radioactive seeds into the prostate.

catheterization—A procedure in which a tube is inserted into the urethra to drain urine from the bladder. Used after prostate surgery and in the treatment of acute urinary retention.

cryotherapy—The use of extreme cold to treat a disease such as prostate cancer.

cystoscopy—Passage of a cystoscope (a type of telescope) through the urethra into the bladder to directly view the urethra and bladder.

digital rectal exam—An examination in which a doctor inserts a lubricated, gloved finger into the rectum to feel for abnormalities of the prostate and rectum.

dihydrotestosterone—The most potent androgen inside prostate cells; formed from testosterone by the enzyme 5-alpha-reductase.

external beam radiation therapy—A therapy for prostate cancer that uses an X-ray machine to aim high-energy radiation at the prostate.

Foley catheter—A small tube inserted through the urethra that allows urine to drain from the bladder into a bag. Has a balloon at its tip so that it remains in place when filled with water.

follicle-stimulating hormone—A pituitary hormone that stimulates sperm production by the testicles.

glandular cells—Cells in the prostate that produce part of the fluid portion of semen.

Gleason score—A classification system for prostate cancer, based on the microscopic appearance of cancer cells; it is used to predict the seriousness of the cancer and the need for treatment. Scores range from 2 to 10. A lower score indicates that the cancer is less aggressive.

hematuria—Blood in the urine.

hormone therapy—Usually a treatment for prostate cancer that has spread beyond the prostate. Slows the progression of cancer by preventing testosterone from acting on cancer cells but does not cure the cancer.

imaging studies—Tests, such as ultrasound, computed tomography (CT), magnetic resonance imaging (MRI), and X-rays that produce an image of the body's insides.

incontinence—An inability to control bladder function.

intermittent androgen suppression—A technique in which androgen blockade with drugs is discontinued once PSA levels fall and is restarted when PSA begins to rise again.

interstitial laser coagulation—A minimally invasive therapy for benign prostatic hyperplasia (BPH); a needle is placed through the urethra to deliver laser energy to the prostate.

Kegel exercises—Exercises to strengthen the pelvic floor muscles. May help men recover bladder function more quickly after prostate surgery.

laparoscopy—A technique in which a tiny instrument containing a light and camera is inserted into the body through a small incision. Used for a variety of surgical and diagnostic procedures, including radical prostatectomy.

laser prostatectomy—A BPH treatment in which laser energy is used to destroy excess prostate tissue.

libido—Sex drive.

luteinizing hormone—A pituitary hormone that stimulates the release of testosterone from the testicles.

luteinizing hormone-releasing hormone (LHRH)—A hormone released by the hypothalamus that stimulates the pituitary gland to produce luteinizing hormone and follicle-stimulating hormone.

luteinizing hormone-releasing hormone analogs—Medications with chemical structures almost identical to natural LHRH. They block the release of luteinizing hormone from the pituitary gland, thus reducing testosterone secretion from the testicles.

medical castration—The use of medication to interfere with the manufacture or actions of testosterone.

metastatic prostate cancer—Prostate cancer that has spread from the prostate to other parts of the body.

nerve-sparing radical prostatectomy—A type of surgery for prostate cancer in which structures important for erectile and bladder function are left intact. Associated with a lower risk of erectile dysfunction and severe incontinence than traditional radical prostatectomy.

neurogenic bladder—Bladder dysfunction related to neurological problems.

nocturia—Frequent nighttime urination; a symptom of benign prostatic hyperplasia (BPH) and other diseases.

orchiectomy—See surgical castration.

palliative therapy—Treatment aimed at relieving pain and limiting disease complications rather than offering a cure.

penile clamp—A device that compresses the penis to prevent urine from leaking.

percent free PSA—The amount of PSA not attached to blood proteins divided by the total amount of PSA. Men with prostate cancer have a lower percentage of free PSA than men with benign prostatic hyperplasia (BPH).

perineal prostatectomy—Type of radical prostatectomy; an incision is made in the perineum instead of the abdomen.

perineum—The area between the scrotum and rectum.

phytotherapy—The use of plant-derived substances to treat a medical condition.

pressure-flow urodynamic studies—Tests that measure bladder pressure during urination by placing a recording device into the bladder and often into the rectum.

ProstaScint—A test for detecting prostate cancer that has spread to other parts of the body (except the bones).

prostate—A gland the size and shape of a crab apple. It surrounds the upper portion of the male urethra and produces part of the fluid that makes up semen.

prostate-specific antigen (PSA)—An enzyme produced by the glandular cells of the prostate and secreted in the seminal fluid released during ejaculation. High blood levels may indicate prostate cancer but can also be caused by benign prostatic hyperplasia (BPH) and infection.

prostatitis—An inflammation of the prostate that may cause pain in the lower back and in the area between the scrotum and rectum.

prostatodynia—Causes the same symptoms as prostatitis but is not associated with infection or inflammation.

PSA density—PSA level divided by size of the prostate. Allows the doctor to better distinguish between benign prostatic hyperplasia (BPH) and prostate cancer by taking prostate size into account when assessing the PSA level.

PSA velocity—A measurement of the changes in PSA values over time. PSA velocity is greater in men with prostate cancer than in those without the disease.

radical prostatectomy—A type of surgery for prostate cancer; removes the entire prostate and the seminal vesicles.

residual urine—Urine retained in the bladder after voiding. It can become infected or lead to the formation of bladder stones.

retrograde ejaculation—Ejaculation of semen into the bladder rather than through the penis.

retropubic open prostatectomy—An operation for benign prostatic hyperplasia (BPH). Used when the prostate is too large for transurethral prostatectomy (TURP). Involves moving aside the bladder so that the inner prostate tissue can be removed without entering the bladder.

seminal vesicles—Glands located on each side of the male bladder that secrete seminal fluid.

simple prostatectomy—A type of surgery for benign prostatic hyperplasia (BPH). Typically involves removing only the inner portion of the prostate and is performed through the urethra (TURP) or an incision in the lower abdomen (retropubic or suprapubic prostatectomy).

smooth muscle cells—Prostate muscle cells that contract to push prostatic fluid into the urethra during ejaculation.

suprapubic open prostatectomy—An operation for benign prostatic hyperplasia (BPH) that is performed when the prostate is too large to allow for transurethral prostatectomy (TURP). Involves opening the bladder and removing the inner portion of the prostate through the bladder.

surgical castration—Surgical removal of either the testicles (bilateral orchiectomy) or the contents of the testicles (subcapsular orchiectomy).

thermotherapy—Treatment for benign prostatic hyperplasia (BPH) that involves heating the prostate. Resulting tissue and nerve damage alleviates symptoms.

TNM system—A system for describing the clinical stage of a cancerous tumor using T numbers to indicate whether the tumor can be felt and, if so, the extent of the tumor. N numbers indicate cancer that has spread to the lymph nodes, and M numbers are used to indicate cancer that has spread to other parts of the body.

total androgen blockade—A treatment for prostate cancer that interferes with the production and action of both testicular and adrenal androgens. Involves combining an antiandrogen with a luteinizing hormone-releasing hormone analog or with surgical castration.

transrectal ultrasound—A procedure that uses an ultrasound probe inserted into the rectum to create images of the prostate. Used during prostate biopsy to diagnose prostate cancer.

transurethral incision of the prostate (TUIP)—A benign prostatic hyperplasia (BPH) treatment in which one or two small incisions are made in the prostate with an electrical knife or laser. Symptoms of BPH are alleviated by decreasing the pressure the prostate exerts on the urethra.

transurethral microwave therapy (TUMT)—A benign prostatic hyperplasia (BPH) treatment that utilizes microwave energy to heat and destroy prostate tissue. The energy is emitted from a catheter inserted in the urethra.

transurethral needle ablation (TUNA)—A treatment for benign prostatic hyperplasia (BPH) in which prostate tissue is destroyed with heat that is delivered by low-energy radio waves through tiny needles at the tip of a catheter inserted into the prostate through the urethra.

transurethral prostatectomy (TURP)—The "gold standard" treatment for benign prostatic hyperplasia (BPH). A long, thin instrument (a resectoscope) is passed through the urethra into the bladder and used to cut away prostate tissue and seal blood vessels with an electric current. Also called transurethral resection of the prostate.

urethra—The canal through which urine is carried from the bladder and out of the body. In men, the urethra also carries semen that is released during ejaculation.

urethral stricture—Narrowing of the urethra.

uroflowmetry—A noninvasive test for benign prostatic hyperplasia (BPH) that measures the speed of urine flow.

vasodilator—A drug that allows the penis to become engorged with blood by widening the blood vessels. Used as a treatment for erectile dysfunction. Examples are alprostadil, papaverine, and phentolamine.

watchful waiting—An approach to managing benign prostatic hyperplasia (BPH) or prostate cancer in which no treatment is immediately attempted, but the patient is carefully monitored. In men with prostate cancer, treatment once initiated is palliative rather than curative.

HEALTH INFORMATION ORGANIZATIONS AND SUPPORT GROUPS

American Cancer Society
☎ 800-227-2345/
866-228-4327 (TTY)
www.cancer.org
National, community-based organization that answers questions about cancer, provides information on specific cancer topics, and makes referrals to treatment centers or self-help organizations. Free publications on prostate cancer. Sponsors a support group called Man to Man.

American Urological Association Foundation
1000 Corporate Blvd.
Linthicum, MD 21090
☎ 866-746-4282/410-689-3700
www.urologyhealth.org
Provides up-to-date doctor-reviewed information on adult and pediatric urological conditions.

Cancer*Care*
275 7th Ave. Floor 22
New York, NY 10001
☎ 800-813-4673
www.cancercare.org
National nonprofit that provides support for patients and families through financial assistance, educational materials, referrals to local community resources, and one-on-one counseling (at the 800 number).

Cancer Information Service
National Cancer Institute
Public Inquiries Office
6116 Executive Blvd., Ste. 300
Bethesda, MD 20892-8322
☎ 800-422-6237/
800-332-8615 (TTY)
www.cancer.gov/aboutnci/cis
Nationwide network that provides information about early detection, risk, and prevention of cancer; local services; and details of ongoing clinical trials. Publishes free literature. Chat online with networkers.

National Kidney and Urologic Diseases Information Clearinghouse
3 Information Way
Bethesda, MD 20892-3580
☎ 800-891-5390/
866-569-1162 (TTY)
www.kidney.niddk.nih.gov
National clearinghouse that provides access to a health information database. Also provides educational material. Write, call, or visit the website for information.

Prostate Conditions Education Council
7009 South Potomac St., Ste. 125
Centennial, CO 80112
☎ 866-477-6788/303-316-4685
www.prostateconditions.org
The Council is a group of doctors and health professionals who produce educational materials on prostate health and are performing research on the detection and treatment of prostate and men's health conditions.

INDEX

NOTES

JOHNS HOPKINS
M E D I C I N E

ARTHRITIS 2012 - Covers the three most common forms of arthritis—osteoarthritis, rheumatoid arthritis and gout—as well as two other rheumatic diseases: fibromyalgia and bursitis.

BACK PAIN and OSTEOPOROSIS 2012 - Addresses back pain due to sprains, strains and spasms, degenerative changes of the spinal bones and disks, disk herniation and spinal stenosis. Also covers osteoporosis—a common cause of fractures in the spine and hip.

CORONARY HEART DISEASE 2012 - Discusses four problems resulting from coronary heart disease: angina, heart attacks, heart failure and arrhythmias.

DEPRESSION and ANXIETY 2012 - Includes major depression, dysthymia, atypical depression, bipolar disorder, seasonal affective disorder, panic disorder, generalized anxiety disorder, obsessive-compulsive disorder, post-traumatic stress disorder and phobias.

DIABETES 2012 - Shows you how to manage your diabetes and avoid complications such as foot problems and vision changes. Reviews the latest tools for monitoring your blood glucose and the newest medications for controlling it.

DIGESTIVE DISORDERS 2012 - Covers gastroesophageal reflux disease, peptic ulcers, dysphagia, achalasia, Barrett's esophagus, esophageal spasm and stricture, gastritis, gallstones, diarrhea, celiac disease, constipation, Crohn's disease, ulcerative colitis and colon cancer.

HEART ATTACK PREVENTION 2012 - Provides up-to-date strategies for preventing a first heart attack, including identifying possible risk factors, the latest screening tests, risk-reducing lifestyle measures and medications for controlling cholesterol.

HYPERTENSION and STROKE 2012 - Explains how to treat your high blood pressure and prevent it from harming you. Also covers the two forms of stroke: ischemic stroke and hemorrhagic stroke.

LUNG DISORDERS 2012 - Includes information on emphysema and chronic bronchitis (together referred to as chronic obstructive pulmonary disease, or COPD), asthma, pneumonia, lung cancer and sleep apnea.

MEMORY 2012 - Tells you how to keep your memory sharp as you get older and how to recognize the symptoms of age-associated memory impairment, mild cognitive impairment and illnesses such as Alzheimer's disease and vascular dementia.

NUTRITION and WEIGHT CONTROL 2012 - Gives you the information you need to eat a healthy diet and keep your weight under control. Also explains what to do when the pounds just don't seem to budge.

PROSTATE DISORDERS 2012 - Helps you decide among the various treatment options for prostate cancer, benign prostatic hyperplasia and prostatitis.

VISION 2012 - Reviews the current knowledge on cataracts, glaucoma, age-related macular degeneration and diabetic retinopathy. Also discusses ways to cope with low vision.

**To order online, visit
JohnsHopkinsHealthAlerts.com/bookstore
or call: 800-829-0422**

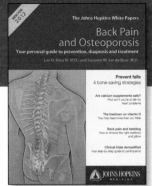

Johns Hopkins
White Papers

Fold along this line and tape closed

Johns Hopkins
Health After 50

Fold along this line and tape closed

Johns Hopkins
Memory Disorders

Fold along this line and tape closed

Johns Hopkins
Prostate Disorders

Fold along this line and tape closed